PATHWAYS

SECOND
EDITION

Reading, Writing, and Critical Thinking

LAURIE BLASS

MARI VARGO

**NATIONAL
GEOGRAPHIC**

L E A R N I N G

Australia • Brazil • Mexico • Singapore • United Kingdom • United States

NATIONAL GEOGRAPHIC
L E A R N I N G

Pathways Foundations
Reading, Writing, and Critical Thinking
Second Edition

Laurie Blass and Mari Vargo

Publisher: Andrew Robinson

Executive Editor: Sean Bermingham

Development Editor: Christopher Street

Director of Global Marketing: Ian Martin

Product Marketing Manager: Tracy Bailie

Media Researcher: Leila Hishmeh

Senior IP Analyst: Alexandra Ricciardi

IP Project Manager: Carissa Poweleit

Senior Director of Production:
   Michael Burggren

Senior Production Controller: Tan Jin Hock

Manufacturing Planner: Mary Beth
   Hennebury

Art Director: Brenda Carmichael

Compositor: MPS North America LLC

Cover Photo: An aerial shot of a sea of
   strawberry greenhouses in Nazilli,
   Turkey: © Leyla Emektar

For product information and technology assistance, contact us at
Cengage Learning Customer & Sales Support, cengage.com/contact
For permission to use material from this text or product,
submit all requests online at **cengage.com/permissions**
Further permissions questions can be emailed to
permissionrequest@cengage.com

Student Book:
ISBN-13: 978-1-337-40775-5

Student Book with Online Workbook:
ISBN-13: 978-1-337-62509-8

National Geographic Learning

20 Channel Center Street
Boston, MA 02210
USA

National Geographic Learning, a Cengage Learning Company, has a mission to bring the world to the classroom and the classroom to life. With our English language programs, students learn about their world by experiencing it. Through our partnerships with National Geographic and TED Talks, they develop the language and skills they need to be successful global citizens and leaders.

Locate your local office at **international.cengage.com/region**

Visit National Geographic Learning online at **NGL.Cengage.com/ELT**
Visit our corporate website at **www.cengage.com**

Printed in China

Print Number: 02   Print Year: 2018

Contents

Scope and Sequence

Critical Thinking	Writing	Vocabulary Extension
Focus Reflecting Synthesizing, Personalizing, Guessing Meaning from Context	**Language for Writing** What is a sentence? Simple present tense of *Be* and other verbs **Writing Goal** Describe yourself and your communication habits.	**Word Forms** Superlative adjectives **Word Web** Social media words
Focus Inferring Personalizing, Synthesizing, Guessing Meaning from Context	**Language for Writing** Using verbs + infinitives Using verb + noun collocations **Writing Goal** Describe your dreams and plans for the future.	**Word Link** Synonyms **Word Web** Time words and phrases
Focus Applying Ideas Synthesizing, Guessing Meaning from Context	**Language for Writing** Using imperative sentences Using *should / shouldn't* **Writing Goal** Write a walking tour of an area you know well.	**Word Partners** Noun + *trip* **Word Web** Prepositions of place and direction
Focus Applying Advice Evaluating, Guessing Meaning from Context	**Language for Writing** Using infinitives of purpose Using *and, but,* and *or* **Writing Goal** Write about what you use the Internet for.	**Word Partners** Verb + *photo* **Word Forms** Nouns and verbs with the same spelling

Scope and Sequence

Critical Thinking	Writing	Vocabulary Extension
Focus Personalizing Synthesizing, Reflecting, Guessing Meaning from Context	**Language for Writing** Using simple present tense (negative) Using adverbs of frequency **Writing Goal** Write about the risks you take.	**Word Link** *-ous* **Word Partners** Nouns/Adjectives + *size*
Focus Analyzing a Sequence Synthesizing, Evaluating, Guessing Meaning from Context	**Language for Writing** Giving reasons Using present continuous tense **Writing Goal** Describe an animal that is in danger.	**Word Forms** Comparative adjectives **Word Partners** Verbs + *about*
Focus Analyzing an Argument Evaluating, Synthesizing, Guessing Meaning from Context	**Language for Writing** Using simple past of *Be* Using simple past of other verbs **Writing Goal** Explain why we should have a day to celebrate a particular inventor.	**Word Forms** Changing verbs to nouns with *-ing* **Word Link** Occupation words ending in *-er* or *-or*
Focus Identifying Speculation Synthesizing, Analyzing an Argument, Guessing Meaning from Context	**Language for Writing** Introducing your opinion Using modal verbs to make predictions **Writing Goal** Express your opinion about the future of space or ocean exploration.	**Word Link** *un-* **Word Link** *-ness*

The Pathway to Academic Readiness

Pathways Reading, Writing, and Critical Thinking, Second Edition uses National Geographic stories, photos, video, and infographics to bring the world to the classroom. Authentic, relevant content and carefully sequenced lessons engage learners while equipping them with the skills needed for academic success. Each level of the second edition features **NEW** and **UPDATED** content.

Academic skills are clearly ▶ labeled at the beginning of each unit.

ACADEMIC SKILLS

READING	Identifying examples
GRAMMAR / WRITING	Using infinitives of purpose
	Using *and, but,* and *or*
CRITICAL THINKING	Applying advice

NEW Reading passages ▶ incorporate a variety of text types, charts, and infographics to inform and inspire learners.

Explicit reading skill instruction ▶ includes main ideas, details, inference, prediction, gist, note-taking, sequencing, and vocabulary development.

▼ **Critical thinking activities** are integrated throughout each unit, and help develop learner independence.

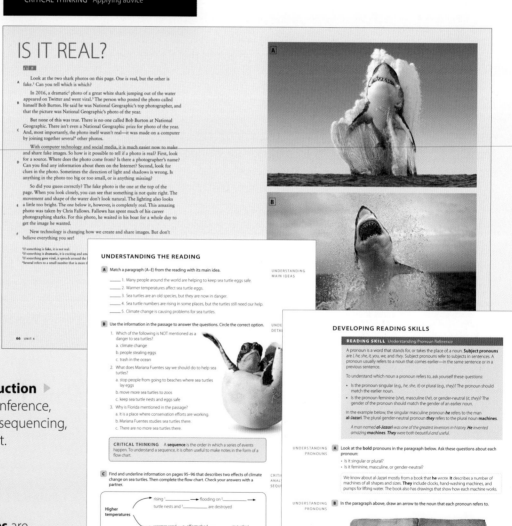

IS IT REAL?

A Look at the two shark photos on this page. One is real, but the other is fake.¹ Can you tell which is which?

In 2016, a dramatic² photo of a great white shark jumping out of the water appeared on Twitter and went viral.³ The person who posted the photo called himself Bob Burton. He said he was National Geographic's top photographer, and that the picture was National Geographic's photo of the year.

But none of this was true. There is no one called Bob Burton at National Geographic. There isn't even a National Geographic prize for photo of the year. And, most importantly, the photo itself wasn't real—it was made on a computer by joining together several⁴ other photos.

With computer technology and social media, it is much easier now to make and share fake images. So how is it possible to tell if a photo is real? First, look for a source. Where does the photo come from? Is there a photographer's name? Can you find any information about them on the Internet? Second, look for clues in the photo. Sometimes the direction of light and shadows is wrong. Is anything in the photo too big or too small, or is anything missing?

So did you guess correctly? The fake photo is the one at the top of the page. When you look closely, you can see that something is not quite right. The movement and shape of the water don't look natural. The lighting also looks a little too bright. The one below it, however, is completely real. This amazing photo was taken by Chris Fallows. Fallows has spent much of his career photographing sharks. For this photo, he waited in his boat for a whole day to get the image he wanted.

New technology is changing how we create and share images. But don't believe everything you see!

¹If something is fake, it is not real.
²If something is dramatic, it is exciting and am
³If something goes viral, it spreads around the I
⁴Several refers to a small number that is more t

66 UNIT 4

UNDERSTANDING THE READING

A Match a paragraph (A–E) from the reading with its main idea.

_____ 1. Many people around the world are helping to keep sea turtle eggs safe.
_____ 2. Warmer temperatures affect sea turtle eggs.
_____ 3. Sea turtles are an old species, but they are now in danger.
_____ 4. Sea turtle numbers are rising in some places, but the turtles still need our help.
_____ 5. Climate change is causing problems for sea turtles.

UNDERSTANDING MAIN IDEAS

B Use the information in the passage to answer the questions. Circle the correct option.

1. Which of the following is NOT mentioned as a danger to sea turtles?
   a. climate change
   b. people stealing eggs
   c. trash in the ocean

2. What does Mariana Fuentes say we should do to help sea turtles?
   a. stop people from going to beaches where sea turtles lay eggs
   b. move more sea turtles to zoos
   c. keep sea turtle nests and eggs safe

3. Why is Florida mentioned in the passage?
   a. It is a place where conservation efforts are working.
   b. Mariana Fuentes studies sea turtles there.
   c. There are no more sea turtles there.

CRITICAL THINKING A **sequence** is the order in which a series of events happen. To understand a sequence, it is often useful to make notes in the form of a flow chart.

C Find and underline information on pages 95–96 that describes two effects of climate change on sea turtles. Then complete the flow chart. Check your answers with a partner.

Higher temperatures
├─ rising ¹_____ → flooding on ²_____
│   turtle nests and ³_____ are destroyed
└─ warmer sand → affects the ⁴_____ in turtles' nests → not enough ⁵_____ turtles are born

DEVELOPING READING SKILLS

READING SKILL Understanding Pronoun Reference

A pronoun is a word that stands for, or takes the place of, a noun. **Subject pronouns** are *I, he, she, it, you, we,* and *they.* Subject pronouns refer to subjects in sentences. A pronoun usually refers to a noun that comes earlier—in the same sentence or in a previous sentence.

To understand which noun a pronoun refers to, ask yourself these questions:
- Is the pronoun singular (e.g., *he, she, it*) or plural (e.g., *they*)? The pronoun should match the earlier noun.
- Is the pronoun feminine (*she*), masculine (*he*), or gender-neutral (*it, they*)? The gender of the pronoun should match the gender of an earlier noun.

In the example below, the singular masculine pronoun *he* refers to the man **al-Jazari**. The plural gender-neutral pronoun *they* refers to the plural noun **machines**.

*A man named **al-Jazari** was one of the greatest inventors in history. **He** invented amazing machines. **They** were both beautiful and useful.*

UNDERSTANDING PRONOUNS

A Look at the **bold** pronouns in the paragraph below. Ask these questions about each pronoun:
- Is it singular or plural?
- Is it feminine, masculine, or gender-neutral?

We know about al-Jazari mostly from a book that **he** wrote. **It** describes a number of machines of all shapes and sizes. **They** include clocks, hand-washing machines, and pumps for lifting water. The book also has drawings that show how each machine works.

UNDERSTANDING PRONOUNS

B In the paragraph above, draw an arrow to the noun that each pronoun refers to.

▶ Pages from al-Jazari's *Book of Knowledge* show one of his water-raising machines.

118 UNIT 7

CRITICAL THINKING **Applying** means using an idea in a new way. For example, if you read an article that gives advice, try to apply that advice to your own situation. This can help you understand the advice better.

Video

Franz Lanting's photo of African elephants in Botswana has been "liked" over a million times on Instagram.

A MILLION "LIKES"

BEFORE VIEWING

A Look at the photo and read the caption. Why do you think this image was so popular?   DISCUSSION

B Read the information about Instagram. Then answer the questions.   LEARNING ABOUT THE TOPIC

Since its launch in 2010, Instagram has become one of the most widely used image-sharing apps in the world. Around 90 percent of Instagram users are under the age of 35. Many of the most popular accounts are held by famous people. Taylor Swift, for example, has over 100 million Instagram followers. Photos of the natural world are also popular. One of the most popular accounts belongs to National Geographic. The photos posted by the organization have been "liked" more than 3 billion times.

1. What kinds of Instagram accounts have the most followers?

   _____

2. What kinds of photos do you think National Geographic posts on Instagram?

   _____

THE VISUAL AGE **63**

◀ **UPDATED** *Video* sections use National Geographic video clips to provide a bridge between Readings 1 and 2, and to give learners ideas and language for the unit's writing task.

◀ **NEW** An additional short reading passage provides integrated skills practice.

▲ **Key academic and thematic vocabulary** is practiced, and expanded throughout each unit.

▲ **NEW Vocabulary extension activities** cover word forms, collocations, affixes, phrasal verbs, and more, to boost learners' reading and writing fluency.

Writing Skills Practice

Pathways' approach to writing guides students through the writing process and develops learners' confidence in planning, drafting, and editing.

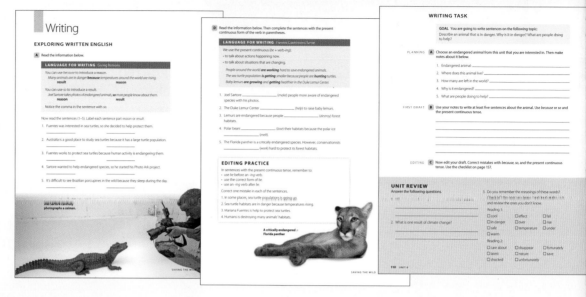

WRITING TASK

GOAL You are going to write sentences on the following topic:
Describe an animal that is in danger. Why is it in danger? What are people doing to help?

Writing Goals and **Language for Writing** sections provide the focus and scaffolding needed for learners to become successful writers.

▼ An **online workbook**, powered by MyELT, includes video clips and automatically graded activities for learners to practice the skills taught in the Student Books.

LANGUAGE FOR WRITING Present Continuous Tense

We use the present continuous (*be* + verb-*ing*):

• to talk about actions happening now.

• to talk about situations that are changing.

People around the world ***are working*** *hard to save endangered animals.*

The sea turtle population ***is getting*** *smaller because people are* ***hunting*** *turtles.*

Baby lemurs ***are growing*** *and* ***getting*** *healthier in the Duke Lemur Center.*

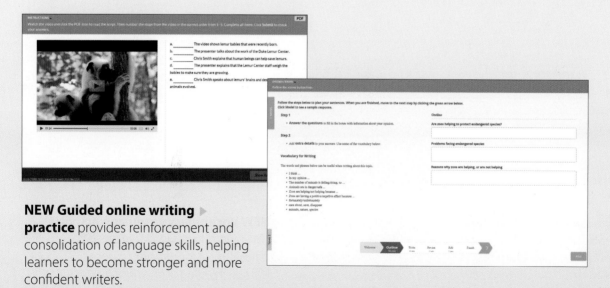

NEW Guided online writing practice provides reinforcement and consolidation of language skills, helping learners to become stronger and more confident writers.

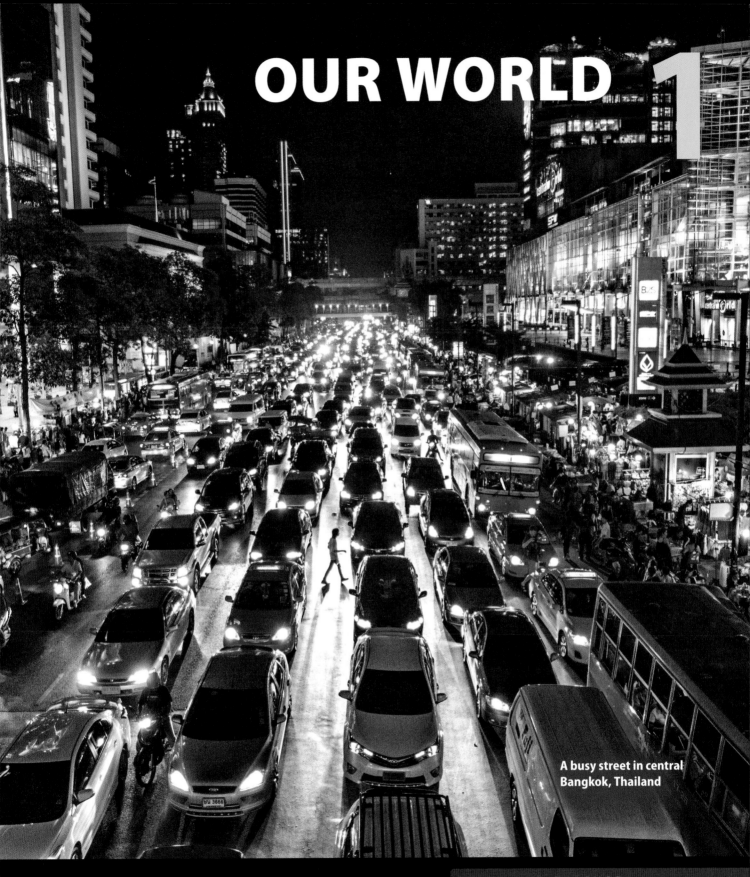

OUR WORLD 1

A busy street in central Bangkok, Thailand

THINK AND DISCUSS

1 How many people do you think are in the world today?
2 Which countries have the most people?

A Look at the information on these pages and answer the questions.

1. What is a megacity?
2. Which is the closest megacity to you?

B Use the correct form of the words in blue to complete the sentences.

Our _____ is the Earth and all the people and things on it.

A _____ is a place like Brazil, Spain, and Japan.

A _____ is a place like Tokyo, New York, and London.

10
New York-Newark, U.S.A.
18.6 million

7
Mexico City, Mexico
21.2 million

Los Angeles-
Long Beach-
Santa Ana, U.S.A.
12.3 million

5
São Paulo, Brazil
21.3 million

Lima, Peru
10.1 million

Rio de Janeiro,
Brazil
13.0 million

Buenos Aires,
Argentina
15.3 million

RISE OF THE MEGACITIES

As the world's population grows, more and more people are living in cities. Many of these people live in megacities—cities with populations of more than ten million. In 1951, there was just one megacity: New York. In 2016, there were 31 megacities in countries all around the world.

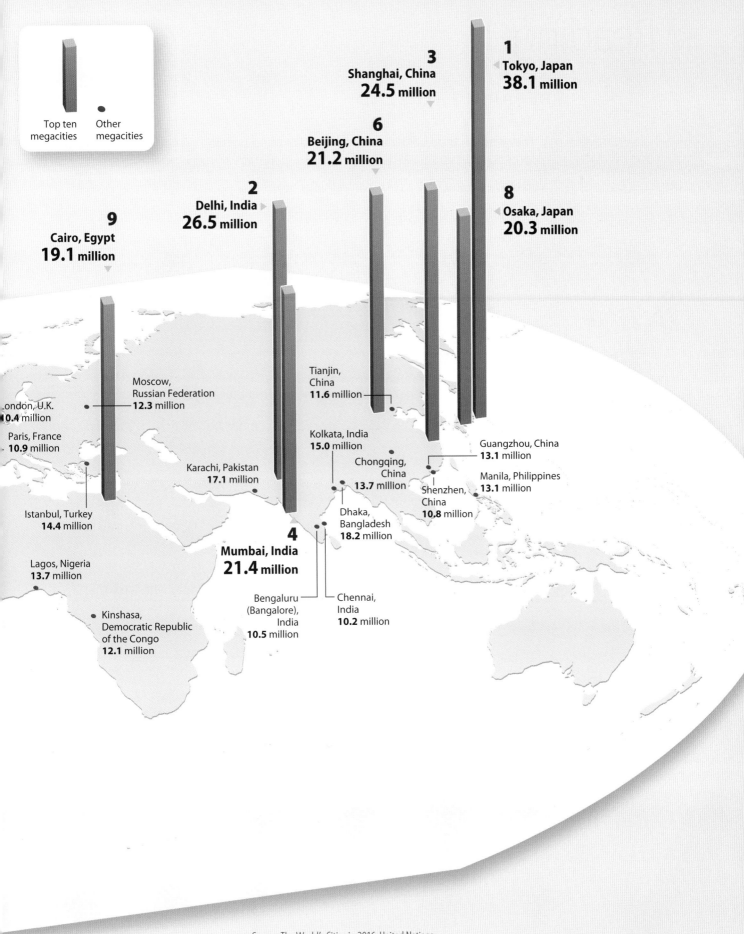

Top ten megacities   Other megacities

1 Tokyo, Japan **38.1 million**

3 Shanghai, China **24.5 million**

2 Delhi, India **26.5 million**

6 Beijing, China **21.2 million**

8 Osaka, Japan **20.3 million**

9 Cairo, Egypt **19.1 million**

London, U.K. **10.4 million**

Paris, France **10.9 million**

Moscow, Russian Federation **12.3 million**

Tianjin, China **11.6 million**

Kolkata, India **15.0 million**

Guangzhou, China **13.1 million**

Istanbul, Turkey **14.4 million**

Karachi, Pakistan **17.1 million**

Chongqing, China **13.7 million**

Shenzhen, China **10.8 million**

Manila, Philippines **13.1 million**

Lagos, Nigeria **13.7 million**

4 Mumbai, India **21.4 million**

Dhaka, Bangladesh **18.2 million**

Kinshasa, Democratic Republic of the Congo **12.1 million**

Bengaluru (Bangalore), India **10.5 million**

Chennai, India **10.2 million**

Source: The World's Cities in 2016, United Nations

Reading 1

PREPARING TO READ

A The words in blue below are used in the reading passage on pages 5–6. Match the sentence parts to make definitions. Use a dictionary to help you.

1. A **restaurant** _____   a. is a place where people stay for a short time.
2. A **job** _____   b. is a place where you buy and eat food.
3. A **hotel** _____   c. is a place away from cities and towns.
4. The **countryside** _____   d. is the work you do to make money.

B Read the definitions. Use the correct form of the words in blue to complete the sentences (1–3).

> If something is **large**, it is big.
> If something **grows**, it becomes bigger.
> If two people or things are **different**, they are not the same.

1. Australia is a very _____ country, but fewer than 25 million people live there.

2. Cities around the world are continuing to _____. There are now 31 cities with a population of over ten million.

3. Shenzhen, China, has changed a lot in the last 50 years. Life there is now very _____ from before.

C List three ideas for each category below. Then share your ideas with a partner.

1. three **cities** you like

   _____   _____   _____

2. three **large** countries

   _____   _____   _____

3. three things you can see in the **countryside**

   _____   _____   _____

D Look up the word *typical* in your dictionary. Then read the title and look at the photos on pages 5 and 6. What do you think the reading is mainly about? Check your prediction as you read the passage.

1. a typical person
2. a typical day on Earth
3. life in a typical city

Holiday travelers pack the Guangzhou Railway Station in Guangdong, China.

THE FACE OF SEVEN BILLION

🎧 1

A   In a **world** of more than seven billion people, is there a "most typical" person? According to statistics, there is. He's a 28-year-old Han Chinese man. He lives in a **city**, can read and write, and probably works in a **hotel** or **restaurant**.

B   There are 1.01 men in the world for every woman, so the typical person is male. China, with over 1.3 billion people, is the **country** with the **largest** population. The largest ethnic group[1] is Han Chinese, and the world's largest age group is 28.

[1]An **ethnic group** is a group of people from one race or culture.

C   More people—51 percent of the world's population—live in a city than in the **countryside**. The most common[2] **job** is in services, such as restaurant and hotel work. Eighty-two percent of the world's population can read and write.

D   What does the typical person look like? Look at the two faces on this page. The pictures were made by researchers at the Chinese Academy of Sciences. They used thousands of photos of 28-year-old Han Chinese men and women. They used them to make images of the typical man and woman on Earth today.

E   What will the typical person be like in the future? The world's population is growing and changing all the time. Every second, five people are born and two people die. In 1800, there were 1 billion people on Earth. Now, there are over 7 billion. By 2045, there may be 9 billion. So the typical person of the future may be very **different** from today.

[2]If something is **common**, it is found in large numbers or happens often.

▼ **Researchers in Beijing created these images of the typical woman and man in the world today.**

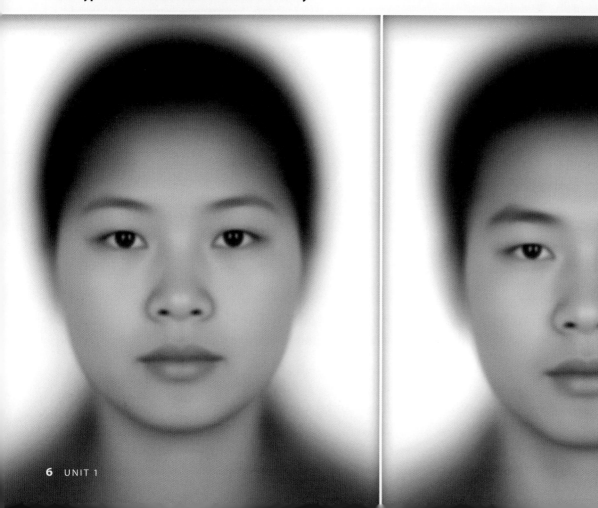

UNDERSTANDING THE READING

A Complete the chart with information about the typical person.

UNDERSTANDING
MAIN IDEAS

	Typical person
1. Lives in a city or the countryside?	
2. Job?	
3. Age?	
4. Male or female?	
5. Country and ethnic group?	

B Complete each sentence (1–5) with the correct numbers from the reading.

UNDERSTANDING
DETAILS

1. About _____ percent of people live in a city.

2. For every woman on Earth, there are _____ men.

3. The population of China is about _____ .

4. The most common age of people living today is _____ .

5. _____ percent of people can read and write.

C Find and underline the following words in the reading. Use the context—the words around the word—to help you understand its meaning. Then match the words to the correct definitions.

CRITICAL THINKING:
GUESSING MEANING
FROM CONTEXT

> **statistics** (paragraph A)   **researchers** (paragraph D)   **images** (paragraph D)

1. A **statistic** _____   a. is a photo or picture.
2. A **researcher** _____   b. is a number used to give information.
3. An **image** _____   c. is a person who finds information about something.

> **CRITICAL THINKING**   When you **reflect** on ideas and information, you connect them with your own experience. Ask yourself these questions as you read: *What do I think about this? How does this relate to my life?*

D Look back at the chart in **A**. Note your answers to the same questions below. How similar are you to the "typical person" described in the passage? Discuss with a partner.

CRITICAL THINKING:
REFLECTING

1. _____   2. _____   3. _____

4. _____   5. _____

DEVELOPING READING SKILLS

> **READING SKILL** Scanning
>
> Scanning helps you find important, or *key*, details quickly. When you scan, you move your eyes quickly over the text and look for specific things. For example, you can look for **numbers** to find times, dates, amounts, ages, and distances. You can also look for **number words** such as *one, two, three, hundred, thousand, million, billion,* and *percent.*

SCANNING **A** Scan the following paragraph and circle all the numbers.

At the moment, China is the country with the largest population. However, many people think that this will change by 2030. India's population is expected to grow to around 1.5 billion by that time, making it the largest in the world. China's population will also grow, but only to around 1.4 billion. The United States will stay as the third largest country, and Indonesia will stay as fourth. In 2015, Brazil had the fifth largest population. But by 2030, it is expected that Nigeria's population will grow to just over 260 million. That will make Nigeria the fifth largest country in the world by population.

SCANNING **B** Now complete the chart using the information in the paragraph above.

Largest countries by population in 2015	Largest countries by predicted population in 2030
1. China (1.38 billion)	1. _____ (1.53 billion)
2. India (1.31 billion)	2. _____ (1.42 billion)
3. United States (322 million)	3. _____ (356 million)
4. Indonesia (258 million)	4. _____ (295 million)
5. Brazil (208 million)	5. _____ (262 million)

SCANNING **C** Scan paragraph E on page 6 and answer the questions.

1. How many people were on the planet in 1800? _____

2. How many people are there now? _____

3. How many people might there be in 2045? _____

4. How many people are born every second? How many people die? _____

Video

Spain and Portugal as viewed from the International Space Station

7 BILLION

BEFORE VIEWING

A What is the population of your country? Is it going up or down? Discuss with a partner.

DISCUSSION

B Look at the information below about the world's population. Then answer the questions.

LEARNING ABOUT THE TOPIC

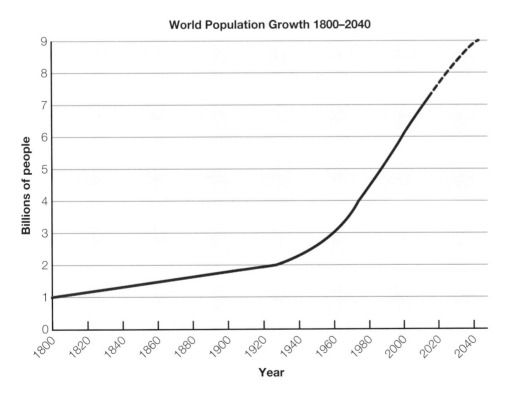

World Population Growth 1800–2040

Billions of people / Year

1. When did the world's population start to grow more quickly?

   _____

2. Why do you think this happened?

   _____

C The words in **bold** below are used in the video. Match each word with the correct definition.

> People in rich countries **consume** most of the world's meat.
> The **average** person born in 2015 will live for 75 years.
> If the population grows too much, some people may not have **adequate** food and water.
> In the future, we will need to use more wind, water, and solar **energy**.

1. _____ (adj) usual, typical, or normal

2. _____ (adj) enough

3. _____ (v) to use, eat, or drink something

4. _____ (n) the power that makes things work

WHILE VIEWING

A ▶ Watch the video. Check (✓) the topics you learn about.

☐ 1. the speed at which the world population is growing

☐ 2. the movement of people from the countryside to the city

☐ 3. the countries that are growing the fastest

☐ 4. differences between rich and poor people in the world

B ▶ Watch the video a second time and complete the sentences.

1. In 2010, the average person lived for _____ years. In 1960, the average person lived for _____ years.

2. In 1975, there were _____ megacities. Now there are _____.

3. Five percent of the population uses 23 percent of the world's _____.

4. Thirteen percent of people don't have _____.

AFTER VIEWING

A The sentences below are from the reading passage on pages 5–6. Check (✓) the sentences that are supported by information in the video.

☐ 1. There are 1.01 men in the world for every woman.

☐ 2. More people … live in a city than in the countryside.

☐ 3. Eighty-two percent of the world's population can read and write.

☐ 4. Every second, five people are born and two people die.

☐ 5. In 1800, there were 1 billion people on Earth.

Reading 2

PREPARING TO READ

A The words in **blue** below are used in the reading passage on pages 12–13. Complete the definitions using the correct form of the words.

pages 12–13

BUILDING VOCABULARY

With **around** 100 million users, LinkedIn is a very **popular** social networking **site**. **However**, it's very different from sites like Facebook. LinkedIn is used mostly by working people. Users **visit** the site to **add** information about their careers and connect with people who have similar jobs. The site also gives **news** about **available** jobs that users might be interested in.

1. If you _____ to something, you make a group of things bigger.

2. If you say a number is _____ one million, it is not exactly one million, but very close.

3. If something is _____ , you can get it or use it.

4. _____ means the same as *but* or *on the other hand*.

5. _____ is information you didn't know before.

6. If something is _____ , many people like it.

7. A _____ is a place on the Internet.

8. If you _____ a place or website, you go there.

B Note answers to the questions below. Then discuss with a partner.

USING VOCABULARY

1. What are the most **popular** social media **sites** in your country?

   _____

2. Do you often read **news** online? Which websites do you use?

   _____

3. Which websites can you **visit** to find out about **available** jobs in your country?

   _____

C Work with a partner. Guess the answers to the questions below. Then scan the reading passage to check your guesses.

PREDICTING

1. What percentage of the world's population uses social media regularly?

   _____

2. How much time does an average person spend on social media each day?

   _____

A CONNECTED WORLD

🎧 2

A   Do you know what your friends watched on TV last night? Do your friends know what you had for breakfast today? Do you think you're using social media too much?

B   Social media is now a part of many people's everyday lives. Estimates[1] suggest that **around** 2.8 billion people use social media regularly. That's almost 40 percent of the world's population. But how much time do we really spend on social media? And what exactly do we spend that time doing?

C   Research shows that, worldwide, the average person spends two hours and 19 minutes on social media each day. People in the Philippines are the most active users. An average person there spends four hours and 17 minutes a day on social media. Research also suggests that women use social media more than men. In the United States, for example, women spend around two hours more per week than men on social media.

D   What do most people do on social media? In general, it seems we spend more time looking at other people's pages than **adding** to our own. According to one survey, the most common social media activities are **visiting** friends' pages, reading their **news**, and commenting on their posts.

E   The most **popular** social media **site** is Facebook, with over 2 billion users. In second place, **however**, is the Chinese site Qzone. In 2017, Qzone was China's most popular social media site, with around 600 million users worldwide. That's more than Twitter and Instagram.

F   Social media continues to grow. Right now, there are five new Facebook profiles every second. And as Internet access[2] becomes **available** to even more people around the world, this growth won't stop anytime soon.

[1]An **estimate** is a good guess based on facts.
[2]If someone has **Internet access**, they are able to connect to the Internet.

The world's most active social media users
(average time spent on social media per day)

Most popular social media sites
(based on the number of users in 2017)

Most common social media activities
(based on 2016 Nielsen Social Media Report)

1 **Philippines**		4h 17m
2 Brazil		3h 43m
3 Argentina		3h 32m
4 Mexico		3h 32m
5 U.A.E.		3h 24m
6 Malaysia		3h 19m
7 Indonesia		3h 16m
8 Egypt		3h 10m
9 Turkey		3h 1m
10 Saudi Arabia		2h 55m

1 Facebook
2 billion users

2 Qzone
632 million

3 Tumblr
550 million

4 Instagram
500 million

5 Twitter
317 million

6 Baidu Tieba
300 million

7 Sina Weibo
297 million

8 Pinterest
150 million

9 YY
122 million

10 LinkedIn
106 million

1 Visiting a friend's page

2 Commenting on a friend's post

3 Sending a message

4 Watching a video

5 Posting a photo

6 "Liking" something

7 Updating your status

8 Updating your profile

9 "Following" someone

10 Playing a game

UNDERSTANDING THE READING

UNDERSTANDING
MAIN IDEAS

A Match each of these main ideas with a paragraph (A–F) from the reading.

_____ 1. Facebook and Qzone are popular social media sites.

_____ 2. The amount of time people spend on social media varies by country and by gender.

_____ 3. On social media, people spend most of their time on friends' pages.

_____ 4. Many people around the world use social media regularly.

INTERPRETING
VISUAL DATA

B Use the reading passage and infographic on pages 12–13 to answer the questions.

1. Which social media sites have 500 million users or more?

   _____

2. In how many countries does the average user spend more than three hours a day on social media?

   _____

3. How many more users did Facebook have than Twitter in 2017?

   _____

4. On social media, is it more common for someone to post a photo or look at a friend's photo?

   _____

CRITICAL THINKING:
GUESSING MEANING
FROM CONTEXT

C Find and underline the following words in the reading on pages 12–13. Use the context—the words around the word—to help you understand their meanings. Complete the definitions.

| **regularly** (paragraph B) | **active** (paragraph C) | **survey** (paragraph D) |

1. If someone is _____ , they are always doing things.

2. If you do a _____ , you find out information by asking people questions.

3. If you do something _____ , you do it often.

CRITICAL THINKING:
PERSONALIZING

D Discuss your answers to these questions with a partner.

1. How much time do you spend on social media?

   _____

2. What do you usually do on social media?

   _____

3. Are your habits similar to or different from the ones in the infographic on pages 12–13?

   _____

Writing

EXPLORING WRITTEN ENGLISH

A Read the information below.

LANGUAGE FOR WRITING What is a Sentence?

A **sentence** is a group of words that expresses an idea. Most types of sentences have at least one subject and one verb. It should begin with a **capital letter** and should end with a **punctuation** mark, such as a period (.), question mark (?), or exclamation point (!).

If a sentence does not have a subject and a verb, it is a **fragment**. Here are two examples. What is missing in each one?

Created a picture of the typical man and woman.
The 28-year-old age group the largest.

Now underline the subject and circle the verb in each sentence (1–5). (Two sentences have more than one subject and verb.)

1. I use my phone every day.
2. My brother and I don't call each other very often.
3. Every day, my friends send me emails or texts.
4. He always goes online when he's watching TV.
5. I connect on my phone when I don't have my laptop.

A young woman checks her cell phone at the Waterfront Promenade in Hong Kong.

B Read the items below (1–7). Check (✓) each complete sentence. If it is a fragment, what is missing? Write **S** for *subject* or **V** for *verb*.

☐ 1. The "most typical" person from China. _____

☐ 2. The population bigger every year. _____

☐ 3. Cell phones are also known as mobile phones. _____

☐ 4. Researchers used thousands of photos of 28-year-old people. _____

☐ 5. Lives in a big city, not a small country town. _____

☐ 6. My school's library has 50 computers for students. _____

☐ 7. I never the computers in the library. _____

C Change the fragments in exercise B into complete sentences using your own ideas.

D Unscramble the words to make sentences. Then underline the subjects and circle the verbs.

1. cell phones / people / A lot of / have / .

_____

2. goes / to the library / every day / My best friend / .

_____

3. all over / Internet / the world / use the / People from / .

_____

4. are / heavy / not very / Tablets / .

_____

E Read the information below. Then complete each sentence (1–6 on page 17) with the correct form of *be*. Use the simple present tense.

LANGUAGE FOR WRITING Simple Present Tense of *Be*

We use the simple present for habits, daily routines, facts, or things that are generally true. The simple present tense of *be* has three forms: *am*, *is*, and *are*.

I	**am / 'm**
he / she / it	**is / 's**
you / we / they	**are / 're**

We usually use nouns, adjectives, or prepositional phrases after *be*.

*I am a **student**.*   *I like Pinterest. It's **fun**.*   *The books are **on the desk**.*

---

1. My favorite social networking site _____ Tagged.

2. My brothers _____ in Seoul.

3. My sister _____ a doctor.

4. I think social media _____ a great way to meet people.

5. Facebook and Twitter _____ fun.

6. I _____ in law school.

F Read the information below.

LANGUAGE FOR WRITING Simple Present Tense of Other Verbs

For verbs other than *be*, use the base form with *I, you, we*, and *they*. For most verbs, use the base form + *-s* with *he, she*, and *it*.

    *I **like** Pinterest.*   *She **likes** Pinterest. We **like** Pinterest.*

    *I **use** Twitter.*   *Mark (or He) **uses** Twitter. Kim and Leo (or They) **use** Twitter.*

If a verb ends in *-y*, drop the *-y* and add *-ies*.

    *I **study** at night.*   *Kay **studies** in the morning.*   *They **study** after lunch.*

Some verbs do not follow the usual rule. You do not use the base form + *-s* with *he, she*, and *it*. Instead, these verbs have irregular forms.

    *She **does** her homework on a tablet.*

    *Alex **goes** to school at 9:00 a.m.*

    *Tomas **has** a laptop, a tablet, and a smartphone.*

Now complete each pair of sentences (1–5) with the correct form of a verb from the box. Use the simple present tense.

like	live	speak	study	use

1. I _____ science for about two hours every day.

    My sister _____ science for about three hours a day.

2. I _____ Twitter better than Facebook.

    Joe _____ Facebook better than Twitter.

3. Pam and Luke _____ in the country.

    Alex _____ in the city.

4. Tina _____ three languages: Spanish, French, and English.

    I _____ two languages: English and Mandarin.

5. Matt and Kim _____ the computers in the library.

    James _____ the computers in the coffee shop.

WRITING TASK

> **GOAL** You are going to write sentences on the following topic:
> Describe yourself and your communication habits.

PLANNING   **A**   Write answers to the questions (1–6). Write notes (not complete sentences). Then share your answers with a partner.

About yourself:

1. Where do you live? _____

2. What languages do you speak? _____

3. Do you have a job? If yes, what is it? If not, what do you want to do?

_____

About your communication habits:

4. How do you connect with friends online? _____

5. How long do you spend on social media in a typical day? _____

6. What websites do you like? _____

FIRST DRAFT   **B**   Use your notes to write four or more sentences about yourself and your communication habits. Use the simple present tense of *be* and other verbs in your sentences.

Example: *I live in Tokyo, Japan.*

EDITING   **C**   Now edit your draft. Correct mistakes with the simple present. Use the checklist on page 157.

UNIT REVIEW

Answer the following questions.

1. What is a megacity?

_____

_____

2. When do you use the simple present tense?

_____

_____

3. Do you remember the meanings of these words? Check (✔) the ones you know. Look back at the unit and review the ones you don't know.

Reading 1:

☐ city	☐ country	☐ countryside
☐ different	☐ grow	☐ hotel
☐ job AWL	☐ large	☐ restaurant
☐ world		

Reading 2:

☐ add	☐ around	☐ available AWL
☐ however	☐ news	☐ popular
☐ site AWL	☐ visit	

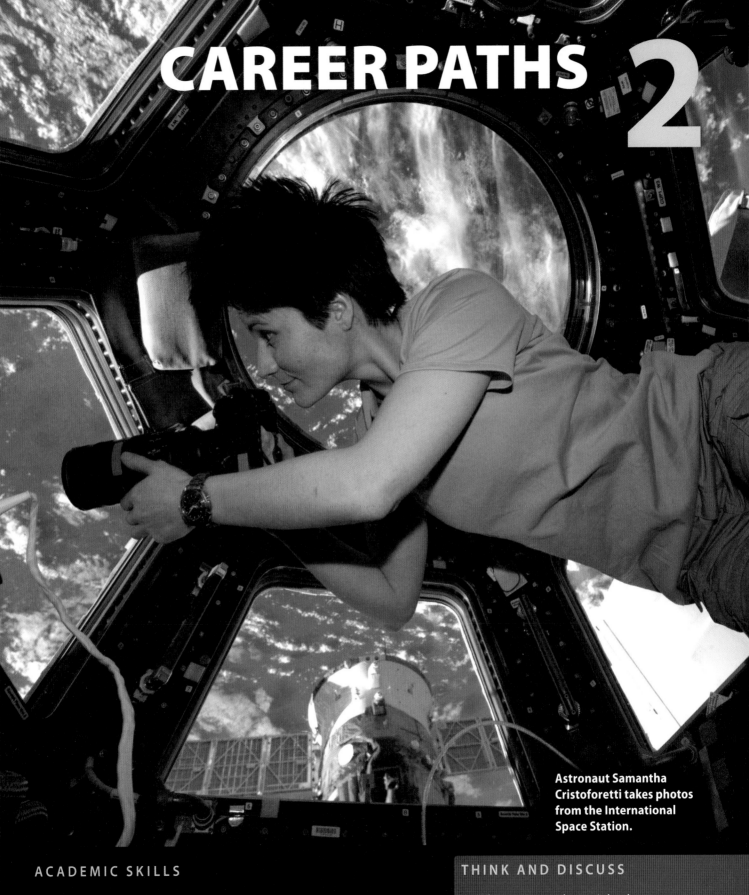

CAREER PATHS

2

Astronaut Samantha
Cristoforetti takes photos
from the International
Space Station.

THINK AND DISCUSS

1 What was your dream job when you were a child?
2 What is your dream job now? Is it different?

EXPLORE THE THEME

A **Look at the information on these pages and answer the questions.**

    1. In which places is engineer the top dream job?

    2. What are the top dream jobs for men and women in the United States?

    3. What percentage of people say that they have their dream job?

B **Match the correct form of the words in blue to their definitions.**

    _____ (n) something you really want to happen

    _____ (adj) wanting to know about something

    _____ (v) to succeed in doing something

DREAM JOBS

What was your **dream** job when you were a child? The website LinkedIn asked 8,000 working people from around the world this question. The top five dream jobs were: engineer, airplane pilot, doctor / nurse, scientist, and teacher.

It also seems that men and women were **interested in** very different jobs as children. In the United States, for example, the top five dream jobs for men were completely different from the dream jobs for women.

But how many people actually **achieved** their dream job? According to the survey, 30 percent of people have their dream job now, or they have a job that is similar to it.

Top dream jobs in the U.S.

Women	Men
① Teacher	① Athlete
② Veterinarian	② Pilot
③ Writer	③ Scientist
④ Doctor / Nurse	④ Lawyer
⑤ Singer	⑤ Astronaut

Sweden

France

Germany

United Arab Emirates

India

Hong Kong, China

Singapore

Indonesia

South Africa

Australia

New Zealand

Number one dream job (women and men)

Engineer   Pilot   Doctor / Nurse   Scientist   Teacher

Reading 1

PREPARING TO READ

BUILDING
VOCABULARY

A The words in **blue** below are used in the reading passage on pages 24–25. Match each word with its definition.

> A job as an airline pilot is a dream for many people. But if you **plan** to become an airline pilot, here are a few things you should know:
> - It helps to be **smart**, and you also need a good college degree.
> - Training to be a pilot is **expensive**. Some pilots pay more than $100,000 for their training.
> - If you get a job with an airline **company**, you need to **practice** in a simulator for about a month before you can **begin** to fly.
> - The money is good, though. Many airline pilots **earn** over $100,000 a year.

1. _____ (v) to start

2. _____ (n) a business that makes money by selling products or services

3. _____ (v) to receive money for working

4. _____ (adj) costing a lot of money

5. _____ (v) to do something so that you get better at it

6. _____ (adj) able to learn things quickly and easily

7. _____ (v) to think about what you will do in the future

USING
VOCABULARY

B List three ideas for each category below. Then share your ideas with a partner.

1. three jobs where people **earn** a lot of money

   _____   _____   _____

2. three big **companies** from your country

   _____   _____   _____

3. three people who you think are really **smart**

   _____   _____   _____

A Korean Air passenger plane lands in the Czech Republic.

DEVELOPING READING SKILLS

A Look at the picture and read the caption on pages 24–25. Answer these questions: SKIMMING

1. Who is the passage about? _____

2. What job do you think the person has? _____

B Now read the title of the passage on page 24 and answer this question: SKIMMING

Reaching for the sky is an expression that usually means "trying to achieve a goal." What goals do you think Barrington Irving had?

_____

_____

C Next, read the subheads in the passage and answer these questions: SKIMMING

1. How does Barrington Irving feel about flying?

_____

2. Where do you think he wanted to fly?

_____

D Now read the first paragraph. What challenges do you think Irving faced? Note your ideas below. PREDICTING

_____

_____

_____

E Now read the whole passage and check your ideas in **D**.

REACHING FOR THE SKY

3

A In 2007, Barrington Irving became the youngest person to fly solo[1] around the world. He was just 23 years old—and he built the plane himself. How did he achieve this?

A PASSION FOR FLYING

B Irving's interest in flying started when he was 15. He was working in his parents' bookstore in Miami, Florida. One of the customers[2] was a pilot, Gary Robinson. One day, Robinson asked Irving if he was interested in flying. Irving didn't think he was smart enough. But the next day, Robinson took Irving to an airport. He showed Irving inside the cockpit[3] of a Boeing 777. That experience changed Irving's life.

Irving really wanted to fly, but flight school was **expensive**. To achieve his dream, he worked different jobs. He washed airplanes and cleaned swimming pools. At home, he **practiced** flying on a video game. In the end, he **earned** enough money for flight school.

CIRCLING THE WORLD

At flight school, Irving achieved his **dream** of learning how to fly. But he wasn't finished. Next, he **planned** to build his own plane and fly solo around the world.

Barrington Irving and his plane, *Inspiration*

Building the plane was difficult. Irving asked more than 50 **companies** for airplane parts. Most said no, but he kept asking. Three years later, he had parts worth $300,000. Columbia, an airplane company, agreed to build a plane using the parts. Soon, his airplane was ready to fly.

On March 23, 2007, Irving **began** his round-the-world trip. After 97 days—with 145 hours in the air—he landed back in Miami. A cheering crowd of people was there to welcome him.

SHARING THE DREAM

Irving saw many young people in the crowd, and this had a powerful effect on him. He wanted to use his experience to help other young people achieve their own dreams.

"Everyone told me what I couldn't do," says Irving. "They said I was too young, that I didn't have enough money. [But] even if no one believes in your dream," he says, "you have to pursue it."

[1] If you do something **solo**, you do it alone.
[2] **Customers** are people who buy things.
[3] The **cockpit** of a plane is the place where the pilot sits.

EXPERIENCE AVIATION

In 2005, Barrington Irving founded Experience Aviation. The organization uses aviation—the designing, building, and flying of aircraft—to build students' skills in science, technology, engineering, and math. In this way, it hopes to inspire young people to achieve dream jobs in aviation or similar industries.

UNDERSTANDING THE READING

A Which of the following would be the best alternative title for the passage?

a. How to Build Your Own Plane   b. Achieving a Dream   c. Life in Flight School

B Put the events (a–f) in the correct order. Write the correct number (1–6) next to each event.

__3__ a. Irving learned to fly.

_____ b. Irving met Gary Robinson.

_____ c. Irving flew around the world.

_____ d. Irving got the parts for his plane.

_____ e Irving decided to build a plane and fly around the world.

_____ f. Irving went to the airport and saw the inside of an airplane

C Circle the correct options to answer the questions.

1. Why was Gary Robinson important in Irving's life?
   a. He taught Irving how to fly.   b. He got Irving interested in flying.

2. How did Irving get enough money for flight school?
   a. He worked different jobs.   b. He asked a company for money.

3. How did Irving get the parts for his airplane?
   a. He asked many different companies.   b. He built them himself.

4. What is the main aim of Experience Aviation?
   a. to teach people how airplanes work   b. to help young people get a dream job

D Find and underline the following words in the reading on pages 24–25. Use the context to help you understand the meaning.

parts (paragraph E)	**cheering** (paragraph F)	**pursue** (paragraph H)

Write the correct form of each word next to its definition. Check your answers in a dictionary.

1. _____ to try to reach or achieve something

2. _____ to shout happily

3. _____ a piece of a machine

> **CRITICAL THINKING**   **Inferring** means understanding something that the writer does not say directly. When you make inferences about a person, for example, you guess information about that person by the things they do.

E From the reading passage, what can we infer about Barrington Irving's character? Find and underline at least three sentences in the passage that support your opinion.

Video

CAVE SCIENTIST

Geologist Gina Moseley inside a cave in Greenland

BEFORE VIEWING

A Look at the photo and the title of the video. What do you think Gina Moseley's job is like? Discuss your ideas with a partner.

PREDICTING

B Read the paragraph. The words in **bold** are used in the video. Match each word with the correct definition.

VOCABULARY IN CONTEXT

A geologist is someone who studies rocks. It's a **challenging** job, as geologists often travel to **remote** places. By studying rocks, geologists can learn a lot about the past. For example, rocks can tell us about past **climate change**. This information is **valuable** because it helps us understand what might happen in the future.

1. _____ (adj) far away from cities and towns

2. _____ (adj) very useful or important

3. _____ (n) changes in the Earth's weather over time

4. _____ (adj) difficult but interesting

C Read the information about Greenland. Then answer the questions.

Five facts about Greenland
- Greenland is the largest island in the world, but only around 57,000 people live there.
- 15,000 people live in the capital city, Nuuk.
- Greenland is not very green. Around 80 percent of the island is covered in ice and snow.
- From May 25th to July 25th, the sun does not go down in some parts of Greenland.
- It's a difficult place to get around. There are only about 63 kilometers of road in the whole country.

1. Would you like to visit Greenland? Why or why not?

_____

2. Do you think Greenland is a good place for geologists to work? Why or why not?

_____

WHILE VIEWING

A ▶ What does Moseley say about her job? Watch the video once and check (✓) the correct answers.

☐ 1. She goes to places that very few people have visited.

☐ 2. She enjoys the long journey to the caves.

☐ 3. She enjoys working as part of a team.

☐ 4. She's happy that the work she does is important.

B ▶ Watch the video a second time and answer the questions.

1. When did Moseley first become interested in caves?

_____

2. How long does it take to get to the caves?

_____

3. What can the cave rocks tell us about past climate change?

_____

AFTER VIEWING

A Complete the chart with information about Gina Moseley's job.

Good Things	Challenges

B Would you like Moseley's job? Why or why not? Discuss with a partner.

Reading 2

PREPARING TO READ

A The words in **blue** below are used in the reading passage on pages 30–31. Match the correct form of each word to its definition.

BUILDING
VOCABULARY

One day, Canadian street entertainer Guy Laliberté had an **idea**. Would it be **possible**, he wondered, to get all the street entertainers he knew to perform **together** in one big **show**? Laliberté started a company that later became known as Cirque du Soleil, or "Circus of the Sun." The show **soon** became very popular. Now it **travels** to different countries, and is **perhaps** the most famous circus in the world. Millions of people have seen a Cirque du Soleil show, and people often **return** to see the shows many times.

**A circus performer
from Cirque du Soleil**

1. _____ (n) a thought about something
2. _____ (adv) with other people
3. _____ (v) to go back to a place again
4. _____ (adv) in a short time
5. _____ (adv) maybe
6. _____ (v) to move from one place to another
7. _____ (adj) able to be done
8. _____ (n) a performance (e.g., of dance or music)

B Answer the questions. Then share your ideas with a partner.

USING VOCABULARY

1. When was the last time you saw a **show**? What was it?

_____

2. Would you **return** to see the show again? Why or why not?

_____

C Skim the reading passage on pages 30–31. Which of the following best describes Emily Ainsworth? Check your ideas as you read the passage.

PREDICTING

a. a street entertainer who joined Mexico's most famous circus
b. a dancer who started a successful traveling circus in Mexico
c. a photographer who was able to spend time in a Mexican circus

LIFE IN THE RING

A As a child, Emily Ainsworth loved the colorful world of traveling circuses. As she grew older, she also became interested in other cultures. "England is a small country," she says. "I saved up for years . . . so that I could afford to travel abroad."

B Ainsworth had many different jobs to pay for her travels. When she was 16, she had earned enough money to travel to Mexico. The experience changed her life. She fell in love with the country and dreamed that perhaps she could return one day.

C As a 22-year-old, Ainsworth got her chance. She entered a radio competition to think of an interesting travel idea. The winner would go on the journey and make a documentary.[1] Ainsworth's idea was to go to Mexico to learn about the lives of circus workers. To her surprise, she won the competition.

D Mexico has many circuses. One of the smaller ones is Circo Padilla. Soon after arriving in Mexico, Ainsworth met Padilla's ringmaster,[2] Don Humberto. He invited her to visit his circus.

E On her first day in Circo Padilla, one of the dancers could not take part in the show.

Humberto asked Ainsworth if she wanted to be a dancer. Five minutes later, Ainsworth says, she was wearing dancer's clothes. It was, she says, "like a childhood dream come true."

F As a circus dancer, Ainsworth and the other circus workers performed and lived together. She also studied and took pictures of circus life. The days were quiet, but at night, the circus world came alive.

G Ainsworth now has a career as a journalist[3] and photographer. She still has a love for Mexico and returns there when she can. "I still feel like a part of that world," she says.

H Her advice to young people is to follow their childhood dreams. "When you're eight years old," she says, "you know that anything is possible."

[1] A **documentary** is a film or TV show about real people or real situations.
[2] A **ringmaster** is the leader of a circus.
[3] A **journalist** writes for a newspaper or magazine.

Emily Ainsworth (right) with a circus performer in Mexico

A pair of Chilean trapeze artists performs in Circo Atayde, a traveling Mexican circus.

UNDERSTANDING THE READING

A Write the correct paragraph letter (A, B, C, E, F) from the reading next to its main idea.

_____ 1. Ainsworth got the chance to return to Mexico.

_____ 2. Ainsworth performed in the circus and studied circus life.

_____ 3. Ainsworth was interested in learning about other cultures from an early age.

_____ 4. Ainsworth's first trip to Mexico changed her life.

_____ 5. Ainsworth got the chance to be a circus dancer.

B Complete the sentences with details from the reading. Write the correct paragraph letter from exercise **A** next to each detail.

Supporting Idea   **Paragraph**

1. To save money to go to Mexico the first time, Ainsworth _____

_____   _____

2. Ainsworth got the chance to go to Mexico again because she

_____   _____

3. When she was not performing, Ainsworth _____

_____   _____

C Find and underline the following words in the reading. Use the context to help you understand the meaning. Then write the correct form of each word or phrase next to its definition.

> **abroad** (paragraph A)   **performed** (paragraph F)   **came alive** (paragraph F)

1. _____ (v) to dance or sing for other people

2. _____ (v) to become exciting

3. _____ (adv) in or to a different country

D Note answers to the questions below. Then discuss with a partner.

1. In what ways are Barrington Irving and Emily Ainsworth similar?

_____

2. Whose dream would you like to follow more—Irving's or Ainsworth's? Why?

_____

Writing

EXPLORING WRITTEN ENGLISH

A Read the information below.

LANGUAGE FOR WRITING Verbs + Infinitives

When certain verbs are followed by other verbs, the infinitive form (*to* + verb) is used.

Emily Ainsworth **plans to return** to Mexico someday.

He **hopes to save** enough money for college.

We **want to visit** China next year.

I **need to get** a different job.

Verbs that follow *plan, hope, want*, and *need* are usually in the infinitive form. There are many other verbs that follow the same pattern.

Note:

• Infinitive forms do not change—they stay the same for every subject. You never need to add *-s* or *-ing* to an infinitive.

• Always include *to* with the verb.

Now complete the sentences (1–8) with the correct form of the verbs in the box. Use each set of verbs only once.

hope / get	plan / go	plan / graduate	need / take
want / help	need / learn	hope / visit	want / be

1. Many college students _____ a good job after they graduate.

2. We _____ some Spanish before we move to Spain.

3. My sister _____ to flight school because she wants to be a pilot.

4. You and Lisa _____ three more classes.

5. Barrington Irving _____ young people achieve their dreams.

6. My brother _____ from college in three years.

7. I really _____ Mexico someday.

8. He's studying at flight school because he _____ a pilot in the future.

B Talk to your classmates and find someone who *wants*, *hopes*, *plans*, or *needs* to do each of the activities in the chart. Ask for extra information.

Find someone who ...	Name	Extra information
1. wants to learn a new language.		Which language?
2. hopes to become famous one day.		Famous for what?
3. plans to move to another country.		Which country?
4. needs to save money for something.		What for?

Example: A: *Do you want to learn a new language?*

B: *Yes, I do.*

A: *Which language?*

B: *French.*

C Use the information in the chart to write four sentences.

Example: Paul wants to learn French.

_____

_____

_____

_____

EDITING PRACTICE

Read the information below.

In sentences with infinitives, remember:

- Infinitive forms do not change—they stay the same for every subject. You never need to add *-s* or *-ing* to an infinitive.
- Always include *to*.

Find and correct one mistake in each of the sentences (1–5).

1. I want get a job in France this summer.

2. Irving plans to helps young people who want to become pilots.

3. Some chefs need studying another language to work in restaurants overseas.

4. Lara hopes become famous one day.

5. My friend wants to having a party.

LANGUAGE FOR WRITING Verb + Noun Collocations

Collocations are words that go together in phrases. It's a good idea to learn collocations as set phrases.

Here are some collocations for talking about hopes, plans, and dreams:

verbs	nouns
go	*to college / to university*
take	*a class / a vacation*
finish	*school / college*
start	*a new job / a family*
learn	*a language / the piano*
study	*math / French*

D Circle the noun or noun phrase that does NOT collocate with the verb.

1. **go**   a. to flight school   b. to Europe   c. a new job
2. **take**   a. a trip   b. school   c. an exam
3. **finish** a. a language   b. university   c. a project
4. **start**   a. university   b. a business   c. history
5. **learn**   a. a class   b. the guitar   c. how to fly
6. **study**   a. science   b. a class   c. English

E Complete each sentence with a suitable verb. Sometimes more than one verb is possible.

1. To be a doctor, he needs to _____ a medical exam.

2. My sister hopes to _____ a language so she can work overseas.

3. Before I buy a car, I need to _____ how to drive.

4. I hope to be a circus performer in Mexico, so I plan to _____ a class in Spanish.

5. My friend wants to be a pilot, so she plans to _____ to college and study aviation.

6. After he _____ college, my brother wants to _____ a business.

F Correct each sentence below by replacing one word.

1. I hope to take to university after I finish high school.

2. I want to start French when I go to college.

3. My friend plans to go to Asia after he passes university.

4. If I want to pass my math exam, I think I need to study an extra class.

WRITING TASK

> **GOAL** You are going to write sentences on the following topic:
> Describe your plans and dreams for the future.

PLANNING **A** Follow the steps to plan your writing. Make notes in the chart.

Step 1 Write down three dreams or plans that you have for the future.

Step 2 List the things that you need to do to achieve each dream or plan.

My Plan/Dream:	To achieve this, I need to:
1.	
2.	
3.	

FIRST DRAFT **B** Use your ideas above to write three pairs of sentences. In each pair, describe your plan or dream, and explain what you need to do to achieve it. Use *plan*, *want*, *hope*, and *need* and the collocations for achieving dreams.

Example:
I hope to travel around the world after I finish college.
I plan to get a part-time job because I need to save a lot of money.

EDITING **C** Now edit your draft. Correct mistakes with *plan*, *want*, *hope*, and *need* and the collocations for achieving dreams. Use the checklist on page 157.

UNIT REVIEW
Answer the following questions.

1. What was the most interesting job in this unit? Why?

_____

_____

2. What are two collocations with the verb *take*?

_____

3. What are two collocations with the verb *finish*?

_____

4. Do you remember the meanings of these words? Check (✔) the ones you know. Look back at the unit and review the ones you don't know.

Reading 1:

☐ achieve AWL   ☐ begin   ☐ company

☐ dream   ☐ earn   ☐ expensive

☐ interested in   ☐ plan   ☐ practice

☐ smart

Reading 2:

☐ idea   ☐ perhaps   ☐ possible

☐ return   ☐ show   ☐ soon

☐ together   ☐ travel

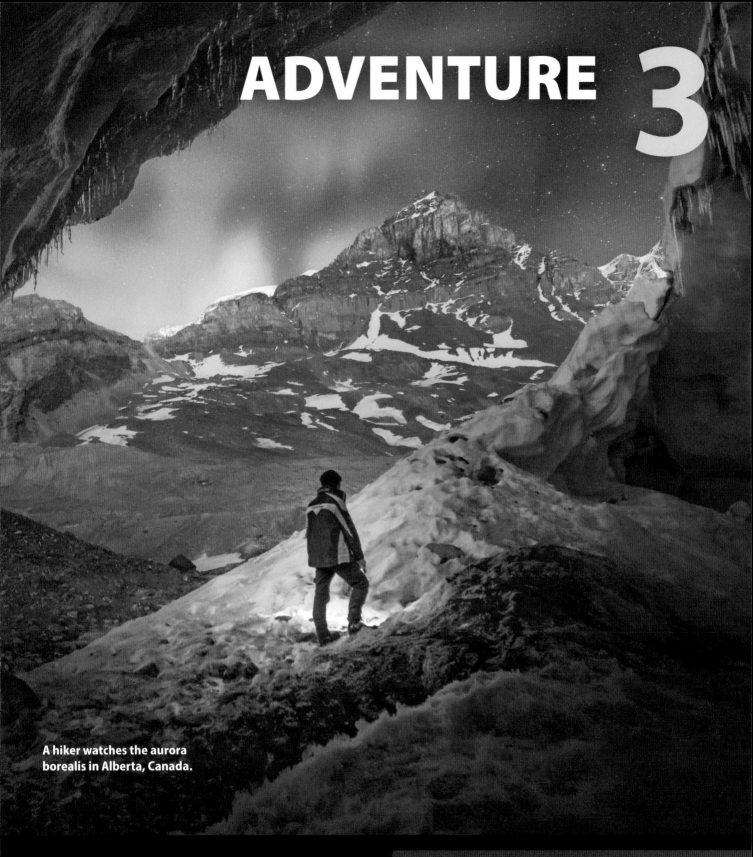

ADVENTURE 3

A hiker watches the aurora borealis in Alberta, Canada.

THINK AND DISCUSS

1 Which place in the world do you most want to visit?
2 What do you want to do there?

A Look at the information on these pages and answer the questions.

1. What age group is this information about?

2. What are three of the places that people in this group want to visit?

B Match the words in blue to their definitions.

_____ (n) a journey or vacation

_____ (n) an exciting experience

_____ (v) to decide on the best option

TRAVEL ADVENTURES

Imagine you could go anywhere in the world for a travel adventure. Which place would you choose? A travel company asked this question to 5,500 millennials—people born between the early 1980s and the early 2000s. The ten most popular choices included famous places like the Egyptian pyramids, the Great Wall of China, and the Eiffel Tower. However, number one on the list was a trip to the Blue Lagoon in Iceland.

❶ Bathe in the Blue Lagoon, Iceland

❷ See the Great Pyramids of Giza

❸ Walk the Great Wall of China

❹ Relax on Byron Bay beach, Australia

❺ Learn how to make pizza in Italy

❻ Drive along Route 66, U.S.A.

❼ Take a gondola ride in Venice, Italy

❽ Climb the Eiffel Tower, Paris

❾ Watch sea turtles in Costa Rica

❿ Enjoy a picnic in the French countryside

Iceland's Blue Lagoon is naturally heated to around 37–40°C. Iceland has become very popular with tourists in recent years. In 2003, there were around 300,000 foreign visitors to Iceland. By 2016, however, this number was around 1.8 million.

Reading 1

PREPARING TO READ

BUILDING
VOCABULARY

A The words in **blue** below are used in the reading passage on pages 41–42. Read the definitions and complete the sentences with the correct form of the words.

> If you go **hiking**, you go on a long—and sometimes difficult—walk in the countryside.
>
> If something is **low-cost**, it is not expensive.
>
> A **map** is a picture of a place that shows roads, mountains, rivers, and other things.
>
> If you travel **across** a place, you go from one side to the other.
>
> **Anywhere** means any place; you say "anywhere" when the place doesn't matter.
>
> If you **climb** something, you go up to the top of it.
>
> If something is **important**, it is special and very useful.

1. When you travel, it is _____ to keep your passport in a safe place.

2. If you go to New York City, you can _____ 354 steps to the top of the Statue of Liberty.

3. You can have a fun adventure almost _____—in a foreign country, in a new city, or even in your hometown.

4. Singapore is a very small country. You can walk _____ it in one day.

5. When you go _____ in a new place, you should take a _____ with you so you don't get lost.

6. If you want a(n) _____ vacation, go somewhere in your home country.

USING
VOCABULARY

B Note your answers to the questions. Then share your ideas with a partner.

1. What are some good places in your country to go **hiking**?

   _____

2. What are some good **low-cost** vacations that you know about?

   _____

BRAINSTORMING

C What words do you think of when you hear the word *adventure*? Write six words below. Then compare your ideas with a partner.

   _____

PREDICTING

D Read the title and photo caption on page 41. What do you think a "microadventure" is? Discuss with a partner. Check your ideas as you read the passage.

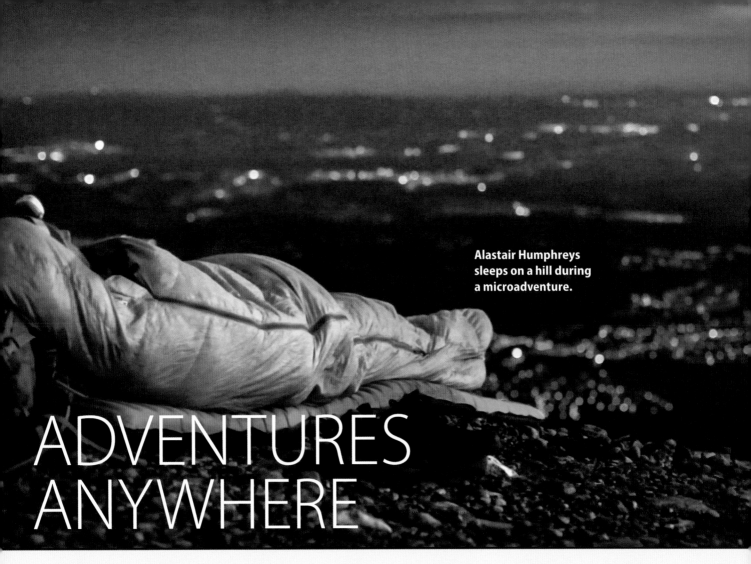

Alastair Humphreys sleeps on a hill during a microadventure.

ADVENTURES ANYWHERE

🎧 5

A   British adventurer Alastair Humphreys has ridden his bike around the world, walked **across** India, and rowed from Africa to South America. In 2011, however, Humphreys had some of the biggest **adventures** of his life—and he never even left the United Kingdom.

B   For a year, Humphreys went on microadventures—small, **low-cost** trips close to home. Why did he do this? "I started to think that it was possible to have an adventure **anywhere**," he explains. For his first trip, he went **hiking** with a friend around the M25—a 188-kilometer road that goes all the way around London. Other adventures included swimming in the River Thames, sleeping outside on a hill, and going on a mountain biking **trip**. Humphreys learned something **important** from his microadventures: We find adventure when we try something new.

C   Humphreys wanted other people to make this discovery, too, so he decided to share his idea. He challenged people to go on microadventures and send him four-minute videos of their trips. He asked them to do things like **climb** a hill, go away for a weekend, or **choose** a random place on a **map** and go there. People from all over the world accepted his challenge and posted their videos on Twitter.

TRY A MICROADVENTURE YOURSELF

Here are six ideas for a microadventure. Why not try one yourself? As Humphreys says, "Life is now or never. Fill it with adventure!"

- Climb a hill that you can see from your town.
- Sleep in your garden for a night.
- Go on a journey to an island.

- Choose a river and travel to where it starts.
- Travel to the coast and sleep there for a night.
- Take a friend on their first microadventure.

"In life it doesn't matter what you do, just that you do something."

Alastair Humphreys

Alastair Humphreys relaxes during a microadventure in the U.K.

UNDERSTANDING THE READING

A What is a microadventure? Check (✓) the best definition.

UNDERSTANDING MAIN IDEAS

☐ a. It's a trip you take by yourself.

☐ b. It's an adventure you have in a foreign country.

☐ c. It's a trip close to home that isn't expensive.

B Which of the following are true about Alastair Humphreys? Check (✓) all that apply.

UNDERSTANDING DETAILS

☐ a. He has had amazing adventures in foreign countries.

☐ b. He believes his biggest adventure was rowing across the Atlantic Ocean.

☐ c. He spent a year having adventures in his home country.

☐ d. His first microadventure was swimming in the River Thames.

☐ e. He challenged people to go on microadventures and make videos of them.

C Find and underline the following words in the reading on pages 41–42. Use the context to help you understand the meaning. Then circle the correct options to complete the sentences.

CRITICAL THINKING: GUESSING MEANING FROM CONTEXT

rowed (paragraph A)   **random** (paragraph C)   **accepted** (paragraph C)

1. If an event is random, it **follows / doesn't follow** a plan.
2. You can row a **boat / car**.
3. If you accept a challenge, you **agree / don't agree** to do it.

> **CRITICAL THINKING**   **Applying** means using an idea in a new way. It can help you understand and remember an idea better. For example, applying Humphreys's idea to your own town can help you understand what he means by "microadventure."

D Work with a partner and discuss your answers to the following questions.

CRITICAL THINKING: APPLYING IDEAS

1. Look at the microadventures listed on page 42. Which of these microadventures can you do where you live?

2. What are some other microadventures you can have in your area? Note your ideas.

_____

_____

_____

DEVELOPING READING SKILLS

READING SKILL Understanding Main Ideas of Paragraphs

The main idea of a paragraph is the most important thing or idea that the writer is saying. A paragraph usually has one main idea. This idea is often introduced in the first or last sentence of the paragraph.

ANALYZING

A Read the paragraph and circle the main idea (a–c).

> There aren't many places better than New Zealand for an adventure holiday. You can try almost any kind of adventure sport, such as surfing, white water rafting, and climbing. New Zealand is also famous for bungee-jumping. One of the first bungee-jumping sites in the world opened in the late 1980s at New Zealand's Kawarau Bridge.

a. Most people visit New Zealand to go bungee-jumping.

b. Surfing is one of the most popular sports in New Zealand.

c. New Zealand is a great place to go for an adventure holiday.

UNDERSTANDING
MAIN IDEAS OF
PARAGRAPHS

B Look again at paragraphs A, B, and C on page 41. Then circle the main idea for each paragraph.

1. Paragraph A

   a. Humphreys's most enjoyable adventure was walking across India.

   b. Some of Alastair Humphreys's biggest adventures were in his home country.

   c. Alastair Humphreys's biggest challenge was rowing from Africa to South America.

2. Paragraph B

   a. Humphreys went on small adventures near his home for a year.

   b. On his first microadventure, Humphreys learned a lot about his friend.

   c. Humphreys's favorite microadventure was swimming in the Thames.

3. Paragraph C

   a. Other people challenged Humphreys to go on microadventures.

   b. Humphreys went on microadventures with other people.

   c. Humphreys challenged other people to go on microadventures.

UNDERSTANDING
MAIN IDEAS OF
PARAGRAPHS

C In which paragraph was the main idea mentioned in the last sentence?

Video

HOOKED ON ADVENTURE

Alastair Humphreys

BEFORE VIEWING

A What do you remember about Alastair Humphreys from the reading on pages 41–42? Note three things you remember about him. Then share your ideas with a partner.

the reading on pages 41–42

BRAINSTORMING

1. _____

2. _____

3. _____

B Read the sentences. The words in **bold** below are used in the video. Match each word with the correct definition.

VOCABULARY IN CONTEXT

Sleeping outdoors can be quite **comfortable** if you have a good tent.

Microadventures are easy to do and not expensive, so there's no **excuse** not to try one.

When I was young, I went on a very **memorable** vacation with my grandparents.

Humphreys loves adventure. In fact, he says he's **hooked on** it.

1. _____ (adj) wanting to do something again and again

2. _____ (adj) easy to remember because it is special or fun

3. _____ (n) a reason you give for not doing something

4. _____ (adj) making you feel relaxed

C Read the information about Alastair Humphreys. Then answer the questions.

In August 2001, Alastair Humphreys rode his bicycle 74,000 kilometers around the world. He traveled through 60 countries, and the whole journey took him four years. By the time he got back, Humphreys was hooked on adventure. He went on other amazing journeys and wrote about his experiences. He continues to write, and also works as a speaker, encouraging people to add more adventure to their lives.

1. How was Humphreys's first adventure different from a microadventure?

   _____

2. What do you think were Humphreys's biggest challenges on his trip round the world?

   _____

WHILE VIEWING

A ▶ Watch the video. Check (✓) the microadventures that Humphreys talks about.

☐ a. sleeping on a hill in another city   ☐ b. going on a journey to an island

☐ c. traveling to the coast   ☐ d. climbing a hill with a group of friends

B ▶ Watch the video again. Answer the questions. Circle the correct option.

1. According to Humphreys, what is the main reason people don't go on adventures?

   a. They think it will be too expensive.

   b. They don't know how to get started.

2. What did Humphreys learn in Hong Kong?

   a. You can have a microadventure even if you live in a big city.

   b. It's important to plan your microadventures carefully.

3. What does Humphreys mean when he says, "Tick-tock, tick-tock, this is our life"?

   a. Life is short, so we should use our time well.

   b. People's lives today are too rushed. We need to relax more.

AFTER VIEWING

A Think about the microadventures in the video and the ones you read about on pages 41–42. Which microadventure would you most like to go on? Note your ideas below. Then discuss with a partner.

Microadventure: _____

Reason: _____

_____

Reading 2

PREPARING TO READ

BUILDING VOCABULARY

A Read the information about San Francisco. The words in blue are used in the reading passage on pages 48–49. Match the correct form of each word with its definition.

> The best way to see San Francisco is to take a walking **tour**. There are many interesting **locations** you can travel to on foot.
>
> When you are in San Francisco, you should **check out** the **Museum** of Modern Art. It's a great place to see the work of some **amazing** modern artists.
>
> There are always **crowds** in Union Square because people like to shop there. There are also a lot of places to eat **nearby**.
>
> Some people think San Francisco is the **capital** of California, but it's actually Sacramento.

1. _____ (n) the city where the government is located

2. _____ (adj) very good, often in a surprising way

3. _____ (n) a place

4. _____ (n) a building where you can look at interesting objects

5. _____ (adv) very close to a particular place

6. _____ (n) a large group of people

7. _____ (n) a trip to see interesting sights

8. _____ (v) to visit or to look at (something)

USING VOCABULARY

B Answer the questions. Then share your ideas with a partner.

1. When did you last go on a **tour** of a city? Where did you go? What did you see?

_____

2. What are the most **amazing** things to see in your country?

_____

3. When did you last go to a **museum**? What did you see there?

_____

BRAINSTORMING

C You are going to read a passage about a tour of the city of London. What do you know about London? What famous locations are there? Share your ideas with a partner.

D Read the passage. Are any of the locations you thought of in **C** mentioned?

A MOVIE-GOER'S GUIDE TO LONDON

🎧 6

A London has been the setting[1] for many popular movies—from James Bond to Harry Potter. So if you are visiting the UK's **capital**, why not follow this walking **tour** and explore some interesting movie **locations**?

B Start at ❶ **the London Film Museum**. Here, you can see a collection of items from many famous movies. The **museum** is near Covent Garden—a famous market. And while you're there, you should **check out** some of the **amazing** street performers.

C Next, walk down King Street, then along New Row to ❷ **J Sheekey**. This restaurant is a great place to see TV and movie stars. And it's not too expensive; you can get a great meal for under £25.

D Nearby is ❸ **Leicester Square**, known as London's "Theatreland." Many famous movie premieres[2] are held in the square, and it is also home to the London Film Festival. One of the exits of the Leicester Square underground station appears in the movie *Harry Potter and the Half-Blood Prince*.

E To get away from the **crowds**, you should spend some time in ❹ **Leicester Square Gardens**. Here, you'll see a statue of William Shakespeare. Shakespeare wrote his most famous plays while he was living in London. Many of his plays, such as *Macbeth*, were later made into movies.

F From Leicester Square, walk down to Charing Cross Road and then to ❺ **the National Gallery**. Here, you can see famous paintings by artists like Vincent van Gogh and Leonardo da Vinci. This museum was also a location in the James Bond movie *Skyfall*.

G Finally, go south on Charing Cross Road, past the underground station—which appears in *Thor: The Dark World*—and follow the Mall. At the end of the Mall, you'll see ❻ **Buckingham Palace**, the home of the British royal family. The palace appears in several movies, such as *The BFG* and *The King's Speech*.

[1]**setting:** the place or area where an event takes place
[2]**premiere:** the first performance of a play or the first showing of a movie

Guards march outside Buckingham Palace.

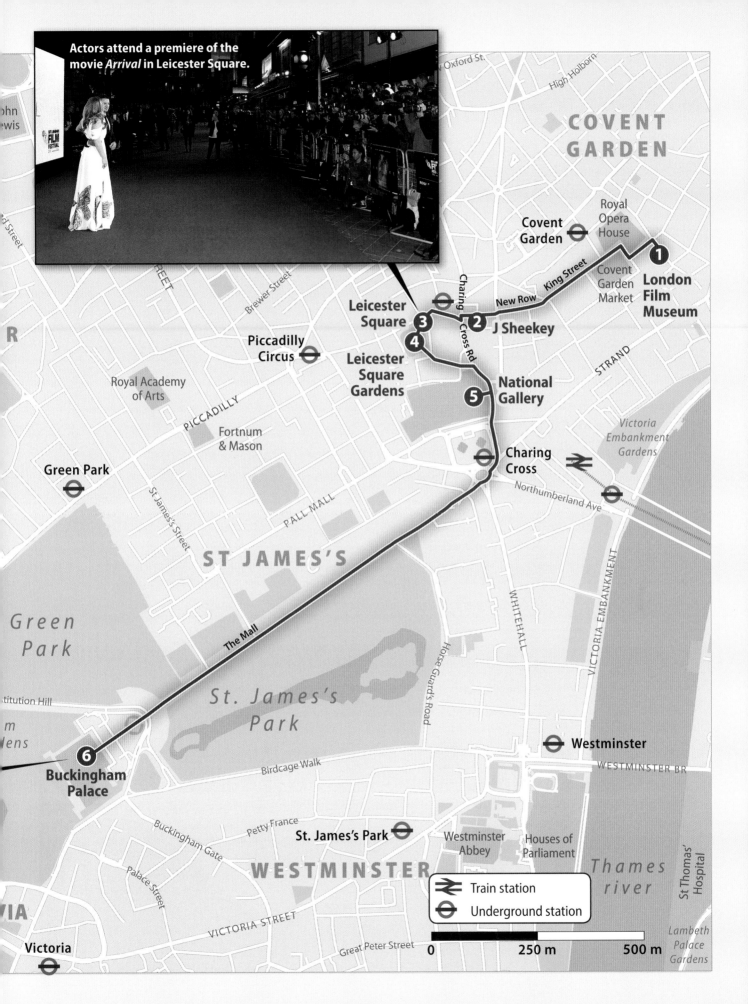

Actors attend a premiere of the movie *Arrival* in Leicester Square.

COVENT GARDEN

Royal Opera House

Covent Garden

Covent Garden Market

1 London Film Museum

King Street

New Row

Charing Cross Rd

2 J Sheekey

Leicester Square

3

4

Piccadilly Circus

Leicester Square Gardens

5 National Gallery

STRAND

Royal Academy of Arts

PICCADILLY

Fortnum & Mason

Green Park

St James's Street

PALL MALL

ST JAMES'S

Charing Cross

Northumberland Ave

Victoria Embankment Gardens

VICTORIA EMBANKMENT

Green Park

titution Hill

ens

The Mall

St. James's Park

6 Buckingham Palace

Birdcage Walk

Buckingham Gate

Petty France

St. James's Park

Palace Street

WESTMINSTER

VICTORIA STREET

Victoria

Great Peter Street

HORSE GUARD'S ROAD

WHITEHALL

Westminster

WESTMINSTER BR

Westminster Abbey

Houses of Parliament

Thames river

St Thomas' Hospital

Lambeth Palace Gardens

| | Train station |
| | Underground station |

0   250 m   500 m

UNDERSTANDING THE READING

UNDERSTANDING PURPOSE

A What kind of person would find the reading passage most useful? Circle the best option.

    a. someone who wants to know the best places to watch movies in London

    b. a visitor to London who is interested in movies and movie stars

    c. a first-time tourist who wants to see the most famous places in London

UNDERSTANDING DETAILS

B Where can you do the following? Match each one with a location (1–6) as labeled on the map.

    1. _____ see a statue of a famous person who wrote plays

    2. _____ see people performing on the street

    3. _____ have some good food for a good price

    4. _____ see some famous paintings

    5. _____ see objects that appeared in movies

UNDERSTANDING DETAILS

C Match each location with the movie in which it appeared. One location is used twice.

    1. *Skyfall* _____

    2. *The BFG* _____

    3. *Thor: The Dark World* _____

    4. *The King's Speech* _____

    5. *Harry Potter and the Half-Blood Prince* _____

    a. Charing Cross Underground Station

    b. Buckingham Palace

    c. the National Gallery

    d. Leicester Square Underground Station

CRITICAL THINKING: APPLYING

D Which type of tour would be best for your town? Check (✓) one on the list or make up your own. Then discuss your ideas with a partner.

☐ a movie tour   ☐ a book tour   ☐ a music tour   ☐ a food tour

☐ a history tour   ☐ an art tour   ☐ _____

▶ **The Mall, leading to Buckingham Palace**

Writing

EXPLORING WRITTEN ENGLISH

A Read the sentences from the reading passages and answer the question below.

1. To get away from the crowds, you <u>should spend</u> some time in Leicester Square Gardens.

2. <u>Sleep</u> in your garden for a night.

3. And while you're there, you <u>should check out</u> some of the amazing street performers.

4. <u>Go</u> on a journey to an island.

5. <u>Choose</u> a river and travel to where it starts.

What do the underlined verbs do?

a. talk about something that happened in the past

b. give the reader reasons

c. tell the reader to do something

LANGUAGE FOR WRITING Using Imperatives and *Should*

You can use the imperative form of verbs when you are giving instructions. The imperative form looks like the base form of a verb. You don't need to put a subject in front of an imperative verb. The subject is understood to be "you."

> ***Climb*** *a hill that you can see from your town.*
> ***Take*** *a friend on their first microadventure.*
> ***Walk*** *down King Street to New Row.*

To make a negative imperative sentence, add *don't* before the verb.

> ***Don't take*** *the subway to the museum. It's quicker if you take a bus.*

You can use the modal verb *should* to give advice or instructions. Use the base form of the verb with *should*.

> *In San Francisco, you **should walk** across the Golden Gate Bridge.*
> *You **should take** a walking tour of Chicago.*

To make a negative statement, use *not* after *should*.

> *You **should not (shouldn't) go** on a bus tour. It's too expensive.*

◀ **San Francisco's Golden Gate Bridge**

B Unscramble the words and phrases to make sentences.

1. right / the street / turn / at the end of / .

   _____

2. at the Haymarket Theatre / should / you / see a play / .

   _____

3. should / you / at a local restaurant / lunch / have / .

   _____

4. the Louvre Museum / the Mona Lisa / at / go / to / see / .

   _____

5. go / afternoon / on / don't / the museum / a Saturday / to / .

   _____

6. you / Rome walking tour / start / at / should / the Trevi Fountain / your / .

   _____

C Complete each sentence (1–7) with the affirmative or negative form of the imperative or *should.*

1. (*try to learn*) _____ the local language before you move to another country.

2. (*travel*) _____ alone in dangerous places.

3. (*carry*) _____ a lot of cash when you're in a busy place.

4. (*study*) _____ hard before you take an exam.

5. (*use*) _____ your cell phone while driving.

6. (*feed*) _____ the animals when you visit a zoo.

7. (*visit*) _____ the Taj Mahal if you go to India.

▶ **The Trevi Fountain, Rome**

D Complete the chart with notes about what a visitor to your town or city should and should not do.

Things You Should Do	Things You Shouldn't Do

Now use your notes to write sentences. Use *should / shouldn't* or an imperative phrase.
Example: If you visit London, you should use the bus to get around.

1. _____
2. _____
3. _____
4. _____
5. _____
6. _____

E Write some directions from your school / university to a place nearby. Use imperatives. Look at the phrases in the box to help you.

Giving Directions
turn left / right (onto George Road)   *go straight*   *cross (the street)*
go past (the supermarket)   *walk down / along (George Road)*

How to get to _____.

1. Go out of this building and turn _____.
2. _____
3. _____
4. _____
5. _____

WRITING TASK

> **GOAL** You are going to write sentences on the following topic:
> Write a walking tour of an area you know well.

PLANNING **A** Follow the steps to plan your writing.

- Think of an area you know well. Make a note of at least three places people should see on a walking tour.
- Make notes on any interesting information about each place—the history, what you can do or see, and other facts.
- Draw a map of the area you chose. Draw a line to show the route of your walking tour. Write numbers on the map to show the places people should visit.

FIRST DRAFT **B** Use your notes to write sentences to describe your walking tour. Use imperatives and *should.*

Start at _____

Information about place A: _____

_____

Introduce place B: *Next,* _____

Information about place B: _____

_____

Introduce place C: *Then* _____

Information about place C: _____

_____

EDITING **C** Now edit your draft. Correct mistakes with imperatives and *should.* Use the checklist on page 157.

UNIT REVIEW

Answer the following questions.

1. What is a microadventure?

_____

_____

2. What are some phrases you can use to give directions?

_____

_____

3. Do you remember the meanings of these words? Check (✔) the ones you know. Look back at the unit and review the ones you don't know.

Reading 1:

☐ across	☐ adventure	☐ anywhere
☐ choose	☐ climb	☐ hiking
☐ important	☐ low-cost	☐ map
☐ trip		

Reading 2:

☐ amazing	☐ capital	☐ check out
☐ crowd	☐ location AWL	☐ museum
☐ nearby	☐ tour	

THE VISUAL AGE

4

A group of people take selfies at the Amman Citadel, Jordan.

THINK AND DISCUSS

1 Do you take a lot of pictures? What do you take pictures of?
2 Do you share pictures online? Which ones?

A Look at the information on these pages and answer the questions.

1. What are some ways that photography has changed since it was invented?
2. Why has the number of photographs taken increased so much in recent years?

B Match the correct form of the words in blue to their definitions.

_____ (n) a picture made with a camera

_____ (v) to put on a website for other people to see

_____ (n) people who use computers, software, or websites

TAKING PICTURES

The graph on this page shows moments in the history of photography. Between 2011 and 2017, more **photos** were taken than in all history before 2011: more than five trillion (5,000,000,000,000).

This huge increase is mainly because of the rise of smartphones and social media. Facebook **users** share over 300 million photos every day, and Instagram users **post** more than 80 million photos a day. It seems that today we really are living in a visual age.

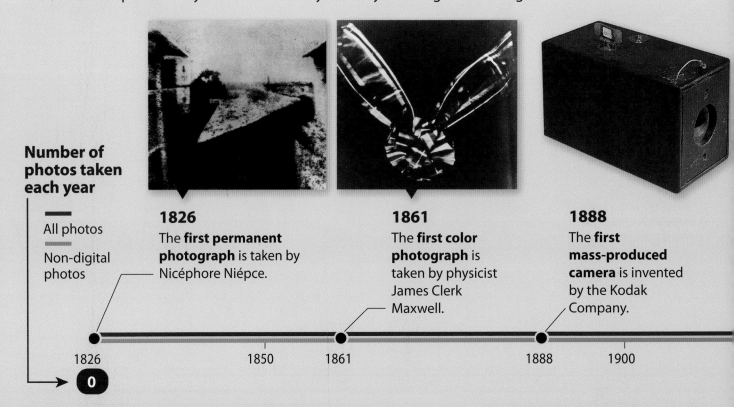

Number of photos taken each year

— All photos

··· Non-digital photos

1826
The **first permanent photograph** is taken by Nicéphore Niépce.

1861
The **first color photograph** is taken by physicist James Clerk Maxwell.

1888
The **first mass-produced camera** is invented by the Kodak Company.

1826   1850   1861   1888   1900

0

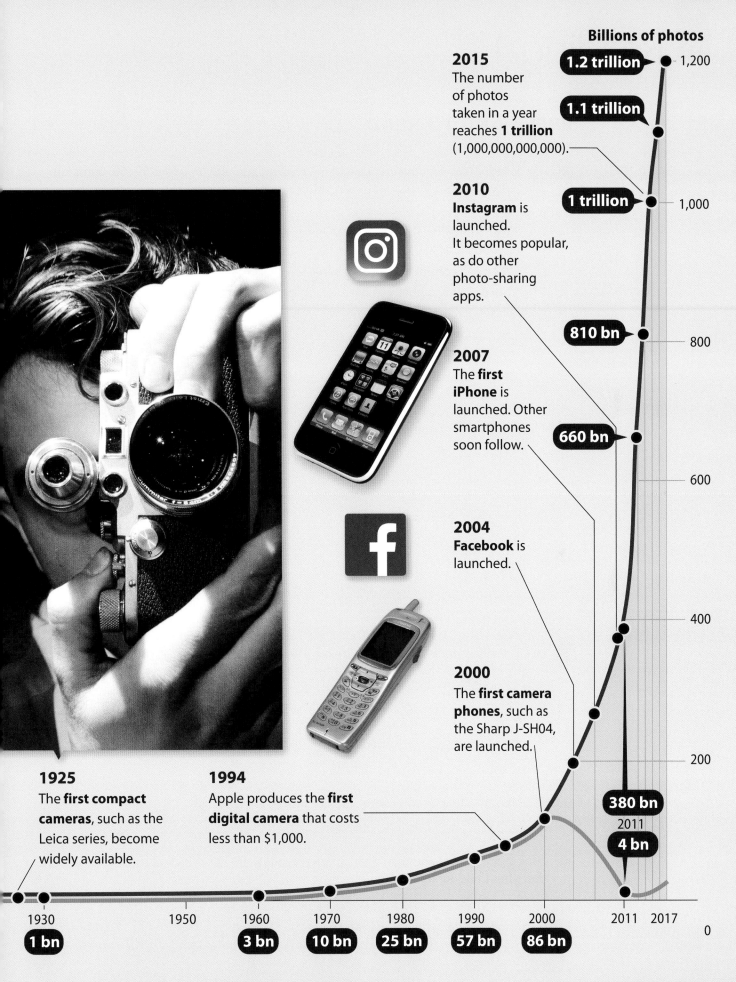

Billions of photos

2015
The number of photos taken in a year reaches **1 trillion** (1,000,000,000,000).

1.2 trillion — 1,200

1.1 trillion

2010
Instagram is launched. It becomes popular, as do other photo-sharing apps.

1 trillion — 1,000

810 bn — 800

2007
The **first iPhone** is launched. Other smartphones soon follow.

660 bn

— 600

2004
Facebook is launched.

— 400

2000
The **first camera phones**, such as the Sharp J-SH04, are launched.

— 200

380 bn
2011

4 bn

1925
The **first compact cameras**, such as the Leica series, become widely available.

1994
Apple produces the **first digital camera** that costs less than $1,000.

1930   1950   1960   1970   1980   1990   2000   2011   2017   0

1 bn   **3 bn**   **10 bn**   **25 bn**   **57 bn**   **86 bn**

Reading 1

PREPARING TO READ

BUILDING
VOCABULARY **A** The words in blue below are used in the reading passage on pages 59–60. Complete the sentences with the correct form of the words.

> When you **join** a group, you become a part of that group.
>
> A **hobby** is an activity you do for fun.
>
> When you **communicate** with someone, you share information.
>
> Your **opinion** is what you think about something.
>
> When you **click on** something, you point at it using your computer mouse and press a button.
>
> When you **contact** someone, you call them or write to them.
>
> When you **find out** something, you learn about it.

1. You can _____ how to do many things on the website wikiHow.

2. Around two billion people have _____ Facebook since it began.

3. Social media has changed the way we _____ with friends and family.

4. I _____ the wrong link and went to a strange website.

5. Many people use social media sites to _____ old friends.

6. Photography is a very popular _____ these days.

7. If you have a(n) _____ about an online article, you can post a comment on it.

USING
VOCABULARY **B** List three ideas for each category below. Then share your ideas with a partner.

1. three popular **hobbies**

   _____   _____   _____

2. three websites you've **joined**

   _____   _____   _____

3. three apps that let you **communicate** with your friends

   _____   _____   _____

PREVIEWING **C** Look at the photos and read the captions on pages 59–60. Which of the following best describes Chris Burkard?

   a. a photographer who became popular on social media

   b. a famous surfer who has many followers on Facebook

   c. a businessman who created the photo-sharing app Instagram

Photos like this, of a surfer in California, have helped Chris Burkard gain a huge following on Instagram.

SHARING SUCCESS

🎧 7

A From a young age, photography was more than just a hobby for Chris Burkard. His amazing photos of surfers in wild locations helped him start a successful career. In 2013, however, something happened that took his career to new heights.

B While on a photography trip in Iceland, a surfer introduced Burkard to a photo-sharing app called Instagram. Burkard decided to join, and started posting images. Four years later, he had over 2 million Instagram followers.

C Photo-sharing sites like Instagram, Imgur, and Flickr are getting more and more popular. In 2011, Instagram had 5 million users. By 2016, that number was 500 million. Sites like these are helping photographers like Burkard connect with a large number of people.

So how do you make a successful photo-sharing account? Here are some tips that might help you become the next Chris Burkard.

1. **Be yourself. Be different.** Don't try to be like anyone else. Create your own unique style.

2. **Get connected.** Share posts from your photo-sharing account on other social media sites. When people see your posts, they might click on them and go to your photo-sharing account.

3. **Choose hashtags carefully.** Look at other accounts to find out which hashtags are popular, and use them. For example, many people use the hashtag #getoutside for photos of the outdoors. There are about 6 million Instagram photos with that hashtag. So if you use it, people who like these 6 million photos will be more likely to find you.

4. **Contact other people.** Follow and comment on other users' posts. When you do this, they are more likely to post comments on yours.

5. **Communicate with your followers.** Make them feel like they are part of a community.[1] For example, ask questions in your captions, and share your own ideas and opinions.

D

[1] A **community** is a group of people who live in the same area or who have similar interests.

Burkard took this photo in the Aleutian Islands, Alaska.

UNDERSTANDING THE READING

A Complete the summary with information from the reading passage.

In ¹_____, Chris Burkard was introduced to the photo-sharing app Instagram.
Burkard already had a successful career in ²_____. He was well-known for his
amazing photos of ³_____. But the photo-sharing app helped take his career
to a new level. By ⁴_____, Burkard had more than 2 million followers. Other
photographers are also finding that image-sharing sites like Instagram, ⁵_____,
and ⁶_____ are helping them connect with a huge audience.

B Check (✓) the advice that the author of the article would agree with.

- ☐ a. Use hashtags that nobody else is using.
- ☐ b. Share your opinions when you post a photo.
- ☐ c. It's a good idea to comment on other people's posts.
- ☐ d. Try to post photos that are different from other people's.
- ☐ e. Use only one social media site to post your photos.

C Find and underline the following words in the reading on pages 59–60. Use the
context to help you understand the meaning. Then write each word next to its
definition.

| **wild** (paragraph A) | **followers** (paragraph B) | **unique** (paragraph D) |

1. _____ (adj) different from everything else
2. _____ (adj) natural, not controlled by people
3. _____ (n) people who receive news and updates about someone
   else on social media

> **CRITICAL THINKING** **Applying** means using an idea in a new way. For
> example, if you read an article that gives advice, try to apply that advice to your own
> situation. This can help you understand the advice better.

D Imagine you are setting up a new Instagram account and want to be successful. Use
your own ideas and the advice given in the article to answer the questions.

1. What would you take photos of?

   _____

2. What website or app would you use to share your photos?

   _____

3. What would make your photos unique?

   _____

4. What hashtags would you use?

   _____

DEVELOPING READING SKILLS

> **READING SKILL** Identifying Examples
>
> Writers use certain words and phrases to introduce examples.
>
> *Social media sites **like** Facebook and Twitter have become popular in many countries.*
>
> *There are several things you can do to take better selfies. **For example**, make sure you are facing the light.*
>
> Remember to use a comma after *For example.*

IDENTIFYING
EXAMPLES

A These sentences are from the reading passage on pages 59–60. Underline the examples.

1. Photo-sharing sites like Instagram, Imgur, and Flickr are getting more and more popular.

2. Choose hashtags carefully. Look at other accounts to find out which hashtags are popular, and use them. For example, many people use the hashtag #getoutside for photos of the outdoors.

3. Communicate with your followers. Make them feel like they are part of a community. For example, ask questions in your captions, and share your own ideas and opinions.

IDENTIFYING
EXAMPLES

B Match the examples (a–e) to the sentences or sentence parts (1–5).

1. There are many search engines you can use, ___

2. You can share many different types of things on social media sites. ___

3. Some of the most popular images on Instagram are of cute animals ___

4. Edit your photos before you post them. ___

5. Hashtags ___

a. For example, you can post photos, videos, text, and links to other websites.

b. like #love, #cute, and #selfie are very popular.

c. like Google and Bing.

d. For example, use photo editing apps that make your pictures look clearer or brighter.

e. like cats or dogs.

IDENTIFYING
EXAMPLES

C Go back to Reading 2 in Unit 3 on page 48. Look at the paragraphs listed below and find:

1. an example of a play written by William Shakespeare (paragraph E)

   _____

2. two examples of artists whose work is in the National Gallery, London (paragraph F)

   _____

3. two examples of movies in which Buckingham Palace appears (paragraph G)

   _____

Video

Franz Lanting's photo of African elephants in Botswana has been "liked" over a million times on Instagram.

A MILLION "LIKES"

BEFORE VIEWING

A Look at the photo and read the caption. Why do you think this image was so popular?

DISCUSSION

B Read the information about Instagram. Then answer the questions.

LEARNING ABOUT THE TOPIC

Since its launch in 2010, Instagram has become one of the most widely used image-sharing apps in the world. Around 90 percent of Instagram users are under the age of 35. Many of the most popular accounts are held by famous people. Taylor Swift, for example, has over 100 million Instagram followers. Photos of the natural world are also popular. One of the most popular accounts belongs to National Geographic. The photos posted by the organization have been "liked" more than 3 billion times.

1. What kinds of Instagram accounts have the most followers?

   _____

2. What kinds of photos do you think National Geographic posts on Instagram?

   _____

C The words in **bold** below are used in the video. Match the correct form of each word with its definition.

> The Asian elephant is an **endangered species**. Not many remain in the wild.
> It's possible to take some great photos at **dawn**.
> A female tiger usually gives birth to three or four **cubs**.

1. _____ (n) the time of day when the sun is coming up

2. _____ (n) a young wild animal, such as a bear or lion

3. _____ (n) a group of animals that could disappear

WHILE VIEWING

UNDERSTANDING
MAIN IDEAS

A ▶ Watch the video. Check (✓) the three things that are true about all the photos in the video.

☐ They are all photos of animals.
☐ They all received over a million "likes" on Instagram.
☐ They were all taken by the same photographer.
☐ They were all posted on National Geographic's Instagram account.

UNDERSTANDING
DETAILS

B ▶ Watch the video again. Match the sentence parts to describe the photos.

1. The photo of the elephants ____   a. was taken in the evening.
2. The photo of the birds ____   b. made the photographer cry.
3. The photo of the leopard ____   c. was taken in the early morning.
4. The photo of the whale ____   d. is part of a project to save endangered species.
5. The photo of the tigers ____   e. shows just a part of the animal.

AFTER VIEWING

REACTING TO
THE VIDEO

A Which photo do you like the best? Why? Discuss with a partner.

REACTING TO
THE VIDEO

B Which photo in the video do you think was most difficult to capture? Why? Note your ideas below and then discuss with a partner.

_____

_____

Reading 2

PREPARING TO READ

A The words in **blue** below are used in the reading passage on pages 66–67. Complete the sentences with the correct form of the words.

BUILDING VOCABULARY

> **direction** (n) the general line that something moves along
>
> **prize** (n) something you receive if you win a competition
>
> **shadow** (n) a dark shape made when you block light
>
> **appear** (v) to become possible to be seen
>
> **believe** (v) to think something is true
>
> **guess** (v) to give an answer or opinion without being sure it is correct
>
> **missing** (adj) not able to be seen or found
>
> **real** (adj) not false or fake

1. Can you _____ which of these two photos is not _____?

2. When taking a photo, it's important to consider the _____ the light is coming from.

3. Your _____ gets longer in the evening when the sun is low in the sky.

4. The police officer showed me a photo of a _____ person he was looking for.

5. The photographer waited for a long time before a shark _____ from below the water.

6. He told me the photo was real, but I didn't _____ him.

7. My friend won a $100 _____ in a photography competition.

B Note answers to the questions below. Then share your ideas with a partner.

USING VOCABULARY

1. Can you remember a photo or piece of news that **appeared** on social media but was not **real**? What was it?

   _____

2. Did you **believe** the story / photo at first, or could you **guess** that it was fake?

   _____

C Read the first paragraph of the reading on pages 66–67. Discuss the question with a partner. Check your ideas as you read the passage.

PREVIEWING

IS IT REAL?

🎧 8

A   Look at the two shark photos on this page. One is **real**, but the other is fake.[1] Can you tell which is which?

B   In 2016, a dramatic[2] photo of a great white shark jumping out of the water **appeared** on Twitter and went viral.[3] The person who posted the photo called himself Bob Burton. He said he was National Geographic's top photographer, and that the picture was National Geographic's photo of the year.

C   But none of this was true. There is no one called Bob Burton at National Geographic. There isn't even a National Geographic **prize** for photo of the year. And, most importantly, the photo itself wasn't real—it was made on a computer by joining together several[4] other photos.

D   With computer technology and social media, it is much easier now to make and share fake images. So how is it possible to tell if a photo is real? First, look for a source. Where does the photo come from? Is there a photographer's name? Can you find any information about them on the Internet? Second, look for clues in the photo. Sometimes the **direction** of light and **shadows** is wrong. Is anything in the photo too big or too small, or is anything **missing**?

E   So did you **guess** correctly? The fake photo is the one at the top of the page. When you look closely, you can see that something is not quite right. The movement and shape of the water don't look natural. The lighting also looks a little too bright. The one below it, however, is completely real. This amazing photo was taken by Chris Fallows. Fallows has spent much of his career photographing sharks. For this photo, he waited in his boat for a whole day to get the image he wanted.

F   New technology is changing how we create and share images. But don't **believe** everything you see!

[1] If something is **fake**, it is not real.
[2] If something is **dramatic**, it is exciting and amazing.
[3] If something **goes viral**, it spreads around the Internet very quickly.
[4] **Several** refers to a small number that is more than two.

UNDERSTANDING THE READING

UNDERSTANDING
THE GIST

A Which of the following would be the best alternative title for the passage?

    a. National Geographic's Best Shark Photos
    b. Don't Believe Everything You See
    c. Famous Photos that Went Viral

UNDERSTANDING
DETAILS

B Read the sentences. Circle **T** for true or **F** for false.

1. Photo A on page 67 was popular on the Internet.	**T**	**F**
2. Bob Burton is the name of a National Geographic photographer.	**T**	**F**
3. Every year, National Geographic gives a prize for photo of the year.	**T**	**F**
4. Photo A on page 67 was made using a computer.	**T**	**F**
5. Chris Fallows has spent a lot of time photographing sharks.	**T**	**F**

UNDERSTANDING
DETAILS

C What are two clues that can help you decide if a photo is real or fake? Note your answers below. Then discuss with a partner.

    1. _____

        For example, _____

    2. _____

        For example, _____

CRITICAL THINKING:
APPLYING

D How can you decide if a news story you see on social media is real or fake? Use the ideas in the passage to help. Note your ideas below. Then discuss with a partner.

_____

_____

_____

_____

CRITICAL THINKING:
EVALUATING

E Note answers to the questions below. Then share your ideas with a partner.

    1. Why do you think people create fake photos or fake news stories?

    _____

    _____

    2. What problems can fake information cause?

    _____

    _____

Writing

EXPLORING WRITTEN ENGLISH

A Read the sentences below and answer the question.

NOTICING

1. He waited in his boat for a whole day <u>to get the image he wanted</u>.

2. Someone put several photos together <u>to create the picture</u>.

3. In the past, people sent their camera film to a shop <u>to get photos printed</u>.

4. Look at other accounts <u>to find out which hashtags are popular</u>, and use them.

What do the underlined words describe?

a. places   b. reasons   c. times

LANGUAGE FOR WRITING Infinitives of Purpose

An infinitive is the base form of a verb starting with *to* (e.g., *to send, to share, to communicate, to find out*). We can use an infinitive of purpose when we want to say *why* or *for what reason* someone does something.

Why do you spend time on social media?

    I spend time on social media **to see** *what my friends are doing and* **to find out** *what is happening in the world.*

Why do you post photos of food?

    I post photos of food **to show** *people what I'm eating.*

You can also start a sentence with an infinitive of purpose. A comma is needed to separate the clauses.

    To chat *with my friends, I use WhatsApp.*

B Match the sentence parts to make full sentences.

1. I use my dictionary app ____   a. to take photos.

2. Many people use Instagram ____   b. to share photos with friends.

3. Most people use their smartphones ____   c. to look up new words.

C Rewrite each sentence in **B** with the infinitive phrase at the start of the sentence.

1. To take photos, _____

2. To share _____

3. _____

D Write answers to the questions using infinitives of purpose. Use your own ideas.

1. Why do most people use social media sites like Facebook?

   _____

2. What app do you use the most? Why do you use it?

   _____

3. Why do you think many people still use email?

   _____

NOTICING **E** Read the sentences and answer the question below.

1. He never thought he would be successful, <u>but</u> he was wrong.
2. Photo-sharing sites like Instagram <u>and</u> Flickr are getting more popular.
3. Is anything in the photo too big <u>or</u> too small?

What is the purpose of the underlined words?

a. to join ideas b. to show cause and effect c. to show the reason for something

---

LANGUAGE FOR WRITING Using *and*, *but*, and *or*

You can connect ideas in a sentence using *and*, *but*, and *or*.
Use *and* to connect two or more items. You can also use *and* to connect two sentences.
Use commas to separate three or more items in a series.
Use a comma to separate two sentences.

> *I use Facebook **and** Twitter to share information.*
> *I use Facebook, Twitter, Instagram, **and** Snapchat to share photos.*
> *I post on Instagram once a day, **and** I post on Imgur once a week.*

Or is used to show two or more choices. Use *or* to connect two or more items in a series or to connect two sentences.

> *Do you prefer to post photos on Facebook **or** Instagram?*
> *Right after I wake up, I usually log on to Facebook, Twitter, **or** Instagram.*
> *I can email the photo to you, **or** I can post it on Instagram.*

But shows two opposite or different ideas. Use *but* to connect two sentences.
Use a comma to separate the two sentences.

> *I like Facebook, **but** I don't like Twitter.*
> *I never post on Facebook, **but** I post a lot on Instagram.*

F Circle the correct conjunction in each sentence.

1. My tablet is useful, **but** / **or** it's quite heavy.

2. I log on to Facebook every day, **and** / **but** I don't often use Twitter.

3. I post photographs on Pinterest **or** / **but** Imgur, **and** / **but** I don't use Instagram.

4. When I wake up, I use my laptop **and** / **or** my tablet—whichever is closer to my bed.

5. I love my car's GPS, **but** / **and** sometimes it gives me the wrong directions.

6. When I ride the bus, I look at Facebook, send emails, **but** / **or** read on my tablet.

7. It's hard to park in the city, so I use an app to find a parking space **but** / **or** I take the subway.

8. I use my dictionary app **but** / **or** go to dictionary.com to look up new words.

G Write a conjunction to complete each sentence. Add commas where they are needed.

1. I post photos _____ videos every day.

2. I bought a new activity tracker to help me get healthier _____ I still don't exercise.

3. In the morning, I always have a cup of tea _____ coffee.

4. Send me an email _____ a text when you get off work.

5. We can order pizza online _____ we'll have to wait a long time before it arrives.

H Combine the sentences using conjunctions. Add commas where they are needed.

1. I use my laptop for work. I use my phone for social media.

   _____

2. Do you prefer Gmail? Do you prefer Yahoo?

   _____

3. Before I buy new technology, I read reviews. I get recommendations from my friends.

   _____

4. I use my phone to listen to podcasts. I use my phone to watch movies. I use my phone to send emails.

   _____

   _____

5. I can use my smartwatch to make phone calls. I prefer to call people on my smartphone.

   _____

6. I comment on people's photos on Facebook. I don't comment on news articles.

   _____

WRITING TASK

GOAL You are going to write sentences on the following topic:
Which websites or apps do you use a lot? What do you use them for?

PLANNING **A** Follow the steps to plan your sentences.

- Brainstorm five apps or websites that you use or visit often. Write them in the chart.
- Make notes about why you use each app or website. Think of two reasons for each.

Website / Name of App	Why?
1.	
2.	
3.	
4.	
5.	

FIRST DRAFT **B** Use your notes to write five sentences about the apps and websites that you use. Use infinitives of purpose and *and, but,* and *or.*

Example: I use WhatsApp to talk to my hockey team and to share pictures of our games.

EDITING **C** Now edit your draft. Correct mistakes with infinitives of purpose and using *and, but,* and *or.* Use the checklist on page 157.

UNIT REVIEW

Answer the following questions.

1. What are two ways to tell if a photo is fake?

_____

_____

2. What are three words that can be used to join ideas in a sentence?

_____

_____

3. Do you remember the meanings of these words? Check (✓) the ones you know. Look back at the unit and review the ones you don't know.

Reading 1:

☐ click on   ☐ communicate **AWL**   ☐ contact **AWL**
☐ find out   ☐ hobby   ☐ join
☐ opinion   ☐ photo   ☐ post
☐ user

Reading 2:

☐ appear   ☐ believe   ☐ direction
☐ guess   ☐ missing   ☐ prize
☐ real   ☐ shadow

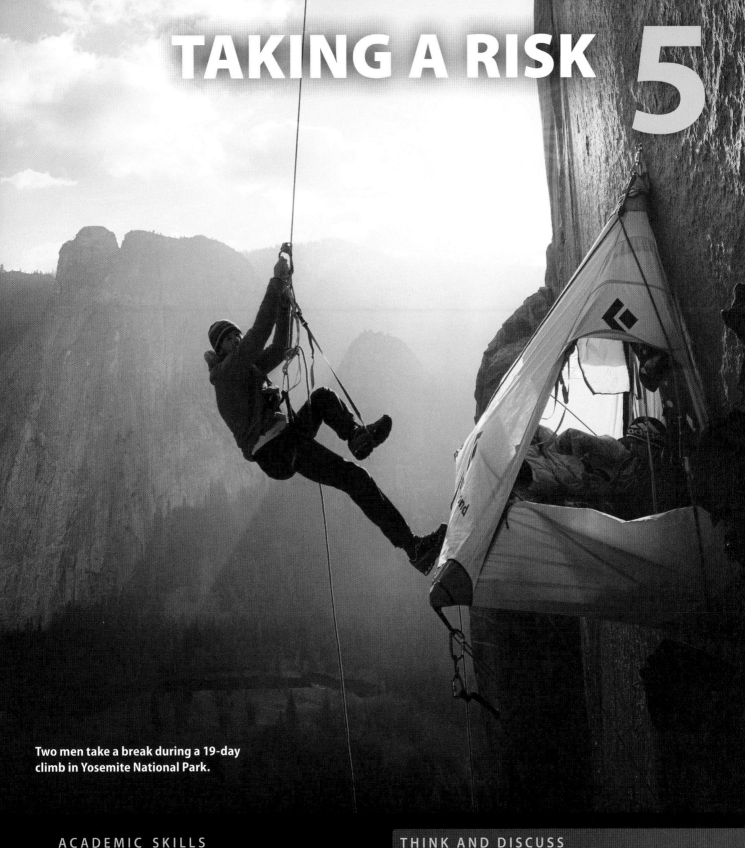

TAKING A RISK 5

Two men take a break during a 19-day
climb in Yosemite National Park.

ACADEMIC SKILLS

READING	Guessing meaning from context
WRITING / GRAMMAR	Using simple present tense (negative)
	Using adverbs of frequency
CRITICAL THINKING	Personalizing

THINK AND DISCUSS

1 "Taking a risk" means doing something dangerous
  or uncertain. What risks do you sometimes take?

2 What kinds of people take a lot of risks in their lives?

A **Look at the information on these pages and answer the questions.**

1. What are the people in the photo doing?
2. Who are more likely to take risks—men or women? Younger people or older people?

B **Use the correct form of the words in blue to complete the definitions.**

If you _____ something, you like doing it.

If something is _____, it is not safe.

Your _____ controls your body.

WHAT IS A RISK-TAKER?

Risk-takers know something bad can happen, but they don't worry about it. A skydiver—a person who jumps from an airplane as a sport—is an example of a risk-taker. It can be **dangerous** to jump from an airplane, of course. But a risk-taker **enjoys** this type of danger.

Psychologists—scientists who study the human **brain**—say that most risk-takers become bored easily. They enjoy the excitement of a risk. Who takes risks? Psychologists say men usually take more risks than women. And the greatest risk-takers are male teenagers.

Skydivers make a star formation above the clouds in Boituva, Brazil.

Reading 1

PREPARING TO READ

A The words in blue below are used in the reading passage on pages 77–78. Match the correct form of each word with its definition.

Mountain climbing can be a dangerous **activity**, but it's also a very popular one. These days, more people than ever are climbing the world's highest peaks, thanks to the growing number of **businesses** that provide professional mountain guides. It's not just the **pleasant** views that people enjoy. What many people love is the experience of going through dangerous **situations**, often feeling **afraid**, but finally **succeeding** in achieving their **goal**.

1. _____ (n) a company that makes money by buying and selling things

2. _____ (n) something you want to achieve, or a reason for doing something

3. _____ (n) the conditions and events happening at a certain time and place

4. _____ (n) something that you spend time doing

5. _____ (adj) nice or enjoyable

6. _____ (adj) worrying that something bad will happen

7. _____ (v) to get the result that you were trying to achieve

B Note answers to the questions below. Then share your ideas with a partner.

1. Do you have a **goal** for learning English? What is it?

   _____

2. When was the last time you felt **afraid**? Why did you feel this way?

   _____

3. Would you like to try any dangerous **activities**? If yes, which ones?

   _____

C Read the title and subheads of the reading passage on pages 77–78. What do you think the reading is mainly about? Check your answer as you read the passage.

a. the risks that professional skiers take
b. new research into risk-taking
c. different types of risk-takers

A ski jumper flies through the air during a tournament in Innsbruck, Austria.

LIVING ON THE EDGE

9

A Some people ski down mountains. Others climb huge rocks or photograph dangerous animals. Why do people enjoy risky activities like these?

THRILL SEEKERS

B Some people take risks simply because it makes them feel good. Psychologist Marvin Zuckerman says that thrill seekers are always looking for change and excitement. When people do something new or risky, a chemical in the brain creates a pleasant feeling. Thrill seekers love this feeling and want to experience it as often as possible.

GOAL-DRIVEN RISK-TAKERS

C Other people don't take risks for the thrill but to achieve a goal. For example, conservationist[1] Mike Fay went on a dangerous 2,000-mile expedition in central Africa. He worked to help save the wildlife there. Fay's expeditions helped create 13 national parks.

[1]A **conservationist** is someone who works to take care of the environment.

PROFESSIONAL RISK-TAKERS

D

For other people, such as extreme athletes,[2] taking risks is part of their job. Sports psychologist Shane Murphy says extreme athletes see the world differently. In a dangerous activity such as skydiving, most people probably do not feel in control.[3] Extreme athletes are different: They feel in control in dangerous situations. The danger can even help them. For example, skier Daron Rahlves says that being afraid makes him try harder to succeed.

EVERYDAY RISK-TAKERS

E

Most of us are not extreme athletes or explorers. However, we still take risks in our lives. Some of us take social risks, such as speaking in front of a large group of people, or talking to people we don't know at a party. Sometimes we take financial risks, such as buying a house. And sometimes we take career risks, such as leaving a job or starting a business. Most people take risks in some areas of life, but not in others. What kind of risk-taker are you?

[2]An **athlete** is someone who is very good at a sport or physical activity.
[3]If you are **in control** of something, you have power over it.

Trading on the stock market is a financial risk that many people take.

UNDERSTANDING THE READING

A Match the sentence parts to complete definitions of the four types of risk-takers.

UNDERSTANDING
MAIN IDEAS

1. A thrill seeker _____
2. A goal-driven risk-taker _____
3. A professional risk-taker _____
4. An everyday risk-taker _____

a. takes many small risks in their daily life.
b. takes risks because it makes them feel good.
c. takes risks as part of their job.
d. takes risks to achieve an aim.

B Answer the questions. Circle the correct options.

UNDERSTANDING
DETAILS

1. Why do people feel good when they take risks?

   a. because the brain releases a chemical
   b. because the heart works faster than usual

2. What was Mike Fay's goal?

   a. to help protect animals in Africa
   b. to help poor people in Africa

3. What does skier Daron Rahlves say about being afraid?

   a. He felt afraid at first but doesn't anymore.
   b. Being afraid helps him in his sport.

C Match the sentence parts to make true statements about the people mentioned in the passage.

IDENTIFYING
EXAMPLES

1. Marvin Zuckerman _____
2. Mike Fay _____
3. Shane Murphy _____
4. Daron Rahlves _____

a. is an example of a goal-driven risk-taker.
b. is an example of a professional risk-taker.
c. believes some people take risks in order to feel good.
d. says extreme athletes cope better with danger than others.

> **CRITICAL THINKING** When you **personalize** something, you take a new idea and apply it to your own situation. It can help you understand and remember an idea better.

D Note answers to the questions below. Then discuss with a partner.

CRITICAL THINKING:
PERSONALIZING

1. Think of a time when you took a risk. What type of risk was it: social, financial, career, or something else? Complete the sentence below.

   I took a _____ risk when I _____

   _____

2. Why did you take the risk? How did you feel afterwards?

   _____

   _____

DEVELOPING READING SKILLS

READING SKILL Guessing Meaning from Context

You can use the context—the words around the word—to guess the meaning of a new word. For example, the context might give the definition, an example, or an explanation that says the same thing with different words. The context can also help you decide the word's part of speech (e.g., noun, verb, adjective).

*Others climb **huge** rocks or photograph dangerous animals.*

The sentence above comes from the reading passage on pages 77–78. We know the passage is about risk, so we can guess that *huge* probably means "very big." We can also guess that the word is an adjective, as it appears before a noun and after a verb.

GUESSING
MEANING FROM
CONTEXT

A Find and underline the following words in the reading on pages 77–78. Write the words next to the correct definitions. Then write the part of speech (e.g., noun, verb, adjective). Check your answers in a dictionary.

create (Paragraph C)	**thrill** (Paragraph C)	**extreme** (Paragraph D)
expedition (Paragraph C)	**social** (Paragraph E)	**financial** (Paragraph E)

1. _____ a trip with a special goal   part of speech: _____

2. _____ relating to groups of people   part of speech: _____

3. _____ relating to money   part of speech: _____

4. _____ a feeling of great excitement   part of speech: _____

5. _____ very far from the average   part of speech: _____

6. _____ to make something new   part of speech: _____

GUESSING
MEANING FROM
CONTEXT

B Read the paragraph below. Then match the words to the correct definitions. Check your answers in a dictionary.

Like many extreme athletes, Emily Cook was a risk-taker from a young age. "I was one of those kids," she says, "who enjoyed and **excelled** at anything **acrobatic**, anything where you were upside down." When she was older, Cook became the U.S. aerials ski champion—a sport where skiers perform acrobatics at great **heights**. "There are definitely moments," she explains, "when you're up there doing a new trick and it seems like the stupidest thing in the world. But **overcoming** that fear is just the coolest feeling."

_____ 1. **excel**   a. (n) a place far above the ground

_____ 2. **acrobatic**   b. (v) to be very good at

_____ 3. **height**   c. (adj) involving difficult physical acts

_____ 4. **overcome**   d. (v) to successfully deal with a problem

Video

Wildlife expert Brady Barr often works with dangerous animals like crocodiles.

KILLER CROCS

BEFORE VIEWING

A Look at the photo and read the caption. What is Brady Barr's job? Why is his job sometimes dangerous?

DISCUSSION

B The words in **bold** are used in the video. Match each word with the correct definition.

VOCABULARY
IN CONTEXT

People who hunt small animals often use **snares**.

Bears and tigers can be **aggressive** if they are frightened.

Rangers know a lot about animals and the environment.

Chimpanzees can **rip** branches off trees and use them as tools.

Conservationists often **rescue** animals that are in danger.

1. _____ (adj) wanting to fight

2. _____ (n) a person who takes care of a forest or a large park

3. _____ (v) to save from danger

4. _____ (v) to tear

5. _____ (n) a trap for catching animals

C Read the information. Complete the notes with your ideas. Then share with a partner.

Nile crocodiles are the largest reptiles on Earth. They live in rivers and swamps in Africa. These enormous animals can grow up to 6 meters in length, and can weigh up to 730 kg. They mainly eat fish, but will attack almost anything nearby, such as zebras, small hippos, birds, and even other crocodiles. They can eat up to half their body weight in one meal.

> Nile crocodiles:
>
> – can be about as long as _____ humans lying end to end
>
> – can weigh around _____ times more than an average human male
>
> – can eat about _____ kg of food in one meal

WHILE VIEWING

A ▶ Watch the video. Answer the questions.

1. Why are the crocodiles in Uganda killing people?
    a. The crocodiles don't have enough food.
    b. People are attacking the crocodiles.
    c. People are feeding the crocodiles.

2. How is Brady Barr helping?
    a. He's catching the crocodiles so they can be trained not to attack humans.
    b. He's trying a new piece of technology used for catching crocodiles.
    c. He's teaching the local rangers to catch and move the crocodiles.

B ▶ Watch the video again. Number the steps from the video in the correct order (1–6)

_____ a. close the crocodile's mouth

_____ b. get close to the crocodile

_____ c. take the crocodile to a new place

_____ d. use the snare to pull the crocodile out

__1__ e. find the crocodile

_____ f. sit on the crocodile's back

AFTER VIEWING

A Would you like to work with dangerous animals? Why or why not? Discuss with a partner.

B Think about the types of risk-takers you read about on pages 77–78. In your opinion, what kind of risk-taker is Brady Barr? Check (✓) more than one option if necessary. Discuss your answer with a partner.

☐ a thrill seeker   ☐ a professional risk-taker
☐ an everyday risk-taker   ☐ a goal-driven risk-taker

Reading 2

PREPARING TO READ

A Read the sentences about climbing. The words in **blue** are used in the reading passage on pages 84–85. Match the correct form of each word with its definition.

BUILDING VOCABULARY

You need **strong** arms and legs to be a good climber.

Many successful rock climbers are **surprisingly** small in terms of their body **size**.

Free soloing is one of the riskiest forms of climbing. It involves climbing in high places **without** any ropes.

Bouldering is another type of climbing. Like free soloing, no ropes are used. But bouldering is safer because if you fall, you're usually quite **close** to the ground.

When climbing indoors, the **difficulty** of different routes is usually marked with different colors. Climbers **follow** the color that matches their ability. Following a route that's too difficult can get you into **trouble**.

1. _____ (n) problems

2. _____ (n) how easy or hard something is

3. _____ (n) how big or small something is

4. _____ (prep) not using or having

5. _____ (adv) used to describe something that wasn't expected

6. _____ (adj) near, not far

7. _____ (adj) having a lot of physical power

8. _____ (v) to move in the same direction as something in front of you

B List three ideas for each category below. Then share your ideas with a partner.

USING VOCABULARY

1. three sports in which you need to be **strong**

   _____   _____   _____

2. three countries that are **close** to your country

   _____   _____   _____

3. three animals that are about the **size** of a small car

   _____   _____   _____

C Read the title and look at the photos on pages 84–85. What do the two people in the passage do? What is risky about these activities? Discuss with a partner.

PREVIEWING

RISK-TAKERS

A
For some people, taking risks is part of their everyday lives. Here are two examples.

Ashima Shiraishi bouldering in Texas, U.S.A.

TEENAGE ROCK CLIMBER

B
Ashima Shiraishi is still in high school, but she's one of the best climbers in the world. In rock climbing, climbers use ropes and other equipment to climb large rocks. In bouldering, participants climb rocks up to six meters high **without** any special equipment, so they have to be very **strong**.

C
Bouldering has **difficulty** ratings from V0 to V16. In 2016, Shiraishi climbed a level V15 boulder called Horizon. She was only the second person to climb it. And at 14 years old, she was also the youngest person, and the first female climber.

D
Shiraishi knows that the sport is dangerous—she once fell more than 10 meters while climbing indoors—but she continues to climb in the most difficult places around the world. Why does she do it? "My dream is to keep on pushing myself, and, maybe, I will push the sport itself," Shiraishi says. "I feel like if people are expecting me to do this, eventually, I will."

UNDERWATER PHOTOGRAPHER

E **Brian Skerry** is an underwater photojournalist. As part of his job, Skerry travels the world and goes diving with dangerous sea animals. To get the best photos, Skerry needs to get as **close** as possible—even if it's dangerous.

F While diving in New Zealand, Skerry found himself swimming next to a right whale. It was the **size** of a city bus. "Nobody is going to believe this," thought Skerry. "I've got to get this picture!" He swam fast so he didn't lose the whale, but he quickly became tired and had to stop. **Surprisingly**, the whale stopped as well. It waited for him and then began to **follow** him around. "It was like swimming around with a friend," Skerry says.

G Why does Skerry take these risks? He hopes his photographs will make people think about life in the world's oceans. "The oceans are in real **trouble**," he says. "As a journalist, the most important thing I can do is to bring awareness."

Brian Skerry's dive partner appears tiny next to a right whale.

UNDERSTANDING THE READING

UNDERSTANDING
MAIN IDEAS

A Complete the diagram according to the information given in the reading passage.

a. takes part in risky activities
b. spends time with dangerous animals
c. travels around the world
d. once had a climbing accident
e. achieved something amazing at a young age
f. works to help the environment

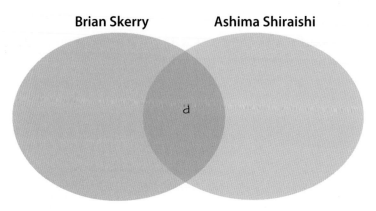

Brian Skerry   **Ashima Shiraishi**

d

UNDERSTANDING
QUOTES

B Answer the questions. Circle the correct option.

1. What is Skerry referring to when he says, "It was like swimming around with a friend"?

   a. his relationship with his dive partner   b. the way a right whale followed him

2. What does Shiraishi mean when she says, "My dream is to keep on pushing myself"?

   a. She will keep trying to climb   b. She needs to become stronger to
      more difficult things.   be successful.

CRITICAL THINKING:
GUESSING MEANING
FROM CONTEXT

C Find and underline the following words in the reading on pages 84–85. Write the words next to their definitions. Then write the part of speech (e.g., noun, verb, adjective). Check your answers in a dictionary.

> **awareness** (paragraph G)   **equipment** (paragraph B)   **participants** (paragraph B)

1. _____ things you need to do a particular activity   part of speech: _____

2. _____ knowing that something is there   part of speech: _____

3. _____ people who join an activity   part of speech: _____

CRITICAL THINKING:
REFLECTING

D Think about the risk-takers in this unit. Which person takes the biggest risks? Why do you think so? Complete the sentence and then share your ideas with a partner.

I think …

☐ Daron Rahlves   ☐ Brian Skerry   ☐ Ashima Shiraishi   ☐ Brady Barr

takes the biggest risks because _____

_____

Writing

EXPLORING WRITTEN ENGLISH

A Read the information in the box.

> **LANGUAGE FOR WRITING** Simple Present Tense (Negative)
>
> We use the simple present for habits, daily routines, facts, or things that are generally true. We use the negative form of the simple present to say what is NOT true.
>
> To form the negative simple present with *be*, add *not* after *be*.
>
> *I'm a skydiver. I **am not** a skier. / I**'m** not a skier.*
> *Daron Rahlves is a skier. He **is not** a skydiver. / He**'s** not a skydiver.*
> *Skiing and skydiving are risky activities. Walking and dancing **are not** risky activities. / Walking and dancing **aren't** risky activities.*
>
> To form the negative simple present with other verbs, use *do + not + verb*.
>
> *I always travel with other people. I **do not** (or **don't**) **like** to travel alone.*
> *Daron Rahlves **does not** (or **doesn't**) **feel** afraid in dangerous situations.*
> *Barr and Skerry take professional risks. They **do not** (or **don't**) have easy jobs.*

Now complete each sentence (1–8) with the negative simple present form of the verb in parentheses.

Example: Risk-takers _____*don't like*_____ *(not like) to be bored.*

1. I _____ (*not enjoy*) going to parties alone.

2. Financial risk-takers _____ (*not be*) afraid to buy stocks.

3. Shiraishi _____ (*not use*) equipment when she climbs boulders.

4. Risk-takers _____ (*not be*) nervous in dangerous situations.

5. The crocodiles in Uganda _____ (*not have*) enough food.

6. My parents _____ (*not agree*) that I should quit my job.

7. Career risk-takers _____ (*not be*) afraid to leave their job.

8. I _____ (*not want*) to work in an office.

Skier Daron Rahlves competing in the Alpine Skiing World Cup

B Rewrite the following sentences (1–6). Change them to negative statements.

Example: Barr avoids dangerous animals.

Barr doesn't avoid dangerous animals.

1. Martin Zuckerman is an extreme athlete.

   _____

2. Most people enjoy dangerous activities.

   _____

3. Most of us are extreme athletes.

   _____

4. I take a lot of risks.

   _____

5. Brian Skerry works in the jungle.

   _____

6. The right whale is a small animal.

   _____

C Write five sentences in your notebook using the negative simple present. Write about things you DON'T do in order to stay healthy.

Example: I don't take the subway to school every day. I sometimes walk.

EDITING PRACTICE

Read the information. Then find and correct one mistake in each of the sentences (1–5).

In sentences with the negative simple present, remember to:

- include the correct form of *be*: *I* **am** *not; he / she / it* **is** *not; we / you / they* **are** *not.*

- use the correct form of *do*: *I / you / we / they* **do** *not; he / she / it* **does** *not.*

- use the base form of the verb after *do + not*. For example: *I don't* **like** *dangerous activities.*

1. I don't wanting to go skateboarding.
2. Most people does not like to take risks.
3. We not enjoy dangerous sports.
4. Brady Barr do not live in Uganda.
5. Good students do not to start studying for a test at the last minute.

D Read the information in the box.

Adverbs of frequency say how often something happens.

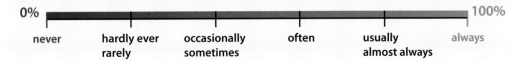

In sentences with *be*, put the adverbs of frequency after *be*. In sentences with other verbs, put the adverb before the verb.

> I'**m never** *late to class. I* **always do** *my homework on time.*
> *She*'**s usually** *careful with money. She* **rarely buys** *stocks.*
> *My children* **aren't always** *careful. They* **sometimes do** *dangerous activities.*

Now put the adverbs of frequency in parentheses in the correct places in the sentences (1–6).

       occasionally
           v
Example: *Teenagers drive too fast. (occasionally)*

1. It's safe to skateboard without a helmet. (*never*)

2. Skydivers wear protective suits. (*almost always*)

3. Skerry meets dangerous sea creatures in his work. (*often*)

4. Surfing is dangerous. (*sometimes*)

5. I take chances with my money. (*rarely*)

6. Shy people talk to strangers at parties. (*hardly ever*)

E How often do you do these activities (1–4)? Discuss your answers with a partner. Then write your answers using adverbs of frequency.

Example: *A: Do you ever travel alone?*
           B: No, I never travel alone. ⟶ *I never travel alone.*

1. travel alone: _____

2. speak in front of large groups: _____

3. talk to strangers at parties: _____

4. study for a test at the last minute: _____

WRITING TASK

GOAL You are going to write sentences on the following topic:
What risks do you take? What risks don't you take?

PLANNING **A** Brainstorm answers to the questions below. Make notes in the chart. Don't write complete sentences.

What are some common risks that people take? Make a list.	
What kinds of risks do you take? Think of at least four examples.	
What kinds of risks do you never take? Think of at least four examples.	

FIRST DRAFT **B** Use your notes above to write three sentences about risks you take and three sentences about risks you don't take. Use adverbs of frequency.

EDITING **C** Now edit your draft. Correct mistakes with the negative simple present and adverbs of frequency. Use the checklist on page 157.

UNIT REVIEW

Answer the following questions.

1. What are two examples of an everyday risk?

_____

_____

2. Which of these is NOT an adverb of frequency?

   a. always   b. quickly   c. usually

3. Do you remember the meanings of these words? Check (✓) the ones you know. Look back at the unit and review the ones you don't know.

Reading 1:

☐ activity   ☐ afraid   ☐ brain
☐ business   ☐ dangerous   ☐ enjoy
☐ goal AWL   ☐ pleasant   ☐ situation
☐ succeed

Reading 2:

☐ close   ☐ difficulty   ☐ follow
☐ size   ☐ strong   ☐ surprisingly
☐ trouble   ☐ without

SAVING THE WILD 6

An endangered sifaka—
a type of lemur

THINK AND DISCUSS

1 Which of the world's animals are disappearing? Why are they disappearing?

2 What can people do to help save animals in danger?

A Read the information below and answer the questions.

   1. What human activities can be dangerous for animals?

   2. Which animal in the photos is most in danger?

   3. What kinds of information does the IUCN use to make its Red List?

B Use the correct form of the words in blue to complete the definitions.

   If something is _____, there is a chance something bad will happen to it.

   The _____ of something is how hot or cold it is.

   If something has a(n) _____ on something else, it changes it.

ANIMALS IN DANGER

Animal species[1] in many parts of the world are **in danger** of becoming extinct.[2] In many cases, the greatest danger is humans. For example, human activity has an **effect** on temperatures around the world. As **temperatures** change, some animals find it difficult to survive. Humans also often build on land where animals live and find food. As a result, many animals lose their homes, or habitats.

The IUCN[3] Red List is a list of animal species that are in danger. The IUCN looks at how many of each animal live in the wild. It also looks at how the population is changing over time. The three highest levels of danger are **Vulnerable**, **Endangered**, and **Critically Endangered**.

[1] A **species** is a type of animal or plant.
[2] If an animal is **extinct**, there are no more left in the world.
[3] International Union for Conservation of Nature

VULNERABLE

Blue crowned pigeons are now only found on the island of New Guinea, in the South West Pacific. Hunting and habitat loss are the main dangers for these beautiful birds.

ENDANGERED

Chimpanzees live in Africa. Their population is falling fast, mainly because of habitat loss. Since the 1970s, the number of chimpanzees has fallen about 50 percent.

CRITICALLY ENDANGERED

There are only between 110 and 130 **blue-throated macaws** left in the forests of Bolivia.

Giant pandas are a small success story for conservation. In 2016, their status on the IUCN Red List changed from Endangered to Vulnerable.

Reading 1

PREPARING TO READ

A The words in blue below are used in the reading passage on pages 95–96. Which of these words are antonyms (words with opposite meanings)? Complete the sentences.

> Polar bear populations continue to **fall** because of climate change.
>
> Camels usually live in **warm** countries like Egypt and Saudi Arabia.
>
> As sea levels **rise**, many animals lose their habitats.
>
> There are just **over** 100 blue-throated macaws left in the wild.
>
> Global warming is most dangerous to animals that prefer **cool** temperatures.
>
> Some scientists believe black rhinos may become extinct in **under** 10 years.
>
> Birds build their nests high in the trees to keep their eggs **safe**.

1. _____ is the opposite of **in danger**.

2. _____ is the opposite of **fall**.

3. _____ is the opposite of **warm**.

4. _____ is the opposite of _____.

B List three ideas for each category below. Then share your ideas with a partner.

1. three countries with a population of **under** 10 million

_____   _____   _____

2. three animals that like to live in **cool** places

_____   _____   _____

3. three things that are **rising** in your country

_____   _____   _____

C You are going to read about sea turtles and how their numbers around the world are falling. What might be causing this? Make a list of possible reasons. Check your predictions as you read the passage.

_____

_____

_____

SEA TURTLES FEEL THE HEAT

🎧 11

A   Sea turtles are some of the oldest species in the world. The first sea turtles lived over 200 million years ago. Today, however, sea turtles are **in danger**. Their numbers are **falling** because of human activities and climate change.

B   Around the world, conservationists are studying the effects of climate change on sea turtles. They believe it affects them in a number of ways. First, sea levels are rising because of higher **temperatures**. As this happens, beach areas become flooded.[1] Sea turtles lay their eggs in the beach sand, so flooding can destroy[2] sea turtle nests and the eggs inside them.

C   Climate change has another effect on the turtles' eggs. In **cooler** temperatures, more male turtles are born. So, as the world becomes **warmer**, more female turtles are born than males. Scientists think that soon there may be no males at all.

[1]If a place is **flooded**, there is a lot of water covering land that is usually dry.
[2]If you **destroy** something, you damage it so badly that it dies or no longer works.

An endangered baby green sea turtle

Mariana Fuentes is a conservationist who works to protect sea turtles.

However, there are people who are trying to help. Conservationists such as Mariana Fuentes study the turtles and work hard to keep them **safe**. "To give marine turtles a better chance," she says, "we have to protect[3] their nesting sites."

D There are now projects in place at many turtle nesting sites around the world. These projects help to protect the turtle eggs from other animals and from humans. Sometimes eggs are also moved to cooler, safer areas.

There are some success stories, too. In the early 1990s, there were fewer than 5,000 green sea turtle nests in Florida. Because of conservation work, this number was up to just **under** 30,000 by 2015. But the turtles still have a lot of challenges, and Fuentes believes that they still need our help.

E "Turtles were here long before humans," she says. "It would be a complete tragedy[4] if they were to become extinct as a result of our actions."

[3]If you **protect** something, you try to keep it safe.
[4]A **tragedy** is a very sad event.

A female green sea turtle, Georgetown, Ascension Island

UNDERSTANDING THE READING

A Match a paragraph (A–E) from the reading with its main idea.

UNDERSTANDING MAIN IDEAS

_____ 1. Many people around the world are helping to keep sea turtle eggs safe.

_____ 2. Warmer temperatures affect sea turtle eggs.

_____ 3. Sea turtles are an old species, but they are now in danger.

_____ 4. Sea turtle numbers are rising in some places, but the turtles still need our help.

_____ 5. Climate change is causing problems for sea turtles.

B Use the information in the passage to answer the questions. Circle the correct option.

UNDERSTANDING DETAILS

1. Which of the following is NOT mentioned as a danger to sea turtles?

    a. climate change

    b. people stealing eggs

    c. trash in the ocean

2. What does Mariana Fuentes say we should do to help sea turtles?

    a. stop people from going to beaches where sea turtles lay eggs

    b. move more sea turtles to zoos

    c. keep sea turtle nests and eggs safe

3. Why is Florida mentioned in the passage?

    a. It is a place where conservation efforts are working.

    b. Mariana Fuentes studies sea turtles there.

    c. There are no more sea turtles there.

A baby sea turtle hatches from its egg.

> **CRITICAL THINKING** A **sequence** is the order in which a series of events happen. To understand a sequence, it is often useful to make notes in the form of a flow chart.

C Find and underline information on pages 95–96 that describes two effects of climate change on sea turtles. Then complete the flow chart. Check your answers with a partner.

CRITICAL THINKING: ANALYZING A SEQUENCE

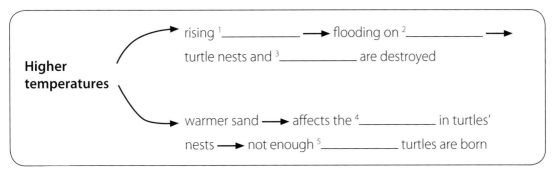

Higher temperatures

rising ¹_____ → flooding on ²_____ → turtle nests and ³_____ are destroyed

warmer sand → affects the ⁴_____ in turtles' nests → not enough ⁵_____ turtles are born

DEVELOPING READING SKILLS

ANALYZING **A** Read the two paragraphs. Circle the words that introduce a reason or a result. Then answer the questions.

Giant pandas became endangered because people began to farm in their habitats. Farming destroyed the pandas' main food source. However, the Chinese government created areas for the pandas to live in, so now they have a better chance of surviving.

1. Why did giant pandas become endangered?

   _____

2. Why do they have a better chance of surviving now?

   _____

Some people kill sea turtles for food. However, since the ocean has dangerous chemicals in it, the turtles' bodies have these chemicals in them, too. People can get sick from eating turtles because of the chemicals in the meat.

1. Why can people get sick from eating sea turtles?

   _____

2. Why are sea turtles' bodies polluted?

   _____

APPLYING **B** Reread the following paragraphs in the reading on pages 95–96. Answer the questions. Then underline the information that gives you the answers.

Paragraph A: Why are sea turtle populations getting smaller?

   _____

Paragraph E: Why is the number of sea turtles in Florida increasing?

   _____

Video

**A lemur at the Duke
Lemur Center, U.S.A.**

SAVING
LEMURS

BEFORE VIEWING

A Look at the photo on this page and the one on page 100. What do you know about these animals? How would you describe them? Discuss with a partner.

DISCUSSION

B Read the information about lemurs. Then discuss these questions.

LEARNING ABOUT
THE TOPIC

Lemurs are primates—like monkeys, gorillas, and humans. There are about 100 species, and they are all found on the island of Madagascar. Lemurs vary in shape and size, from the 9 kg indri lemur to the tiny mouse lemur. Some mouse lemurs weigh just 30 g and are only around 10 cm long. Sadly, lemurs are thought to be the world's most endangered primates. It is believed that 90 percent of all lemur species could become extinct in the next 20 to 25 years.

1. Did any of the information about lemurs surprise you?

_____

2. Why do you think lemurs are endangered?

_____

C The words and phrases below are used in the video. Match each word or phrase with the correct definition.

> If babies **gain weight**, they get bigger. This usually means they are healthy.
>
> To **take care of** baby animals, people keep them warm and give them food.
>
> Gorillas and chimpanzees are close **relatives**. They are both a type of ape.
>
> It's important to **make sure** that baby animals eat good food and are healthy.

1. _____ (v) to become heavier

2. _____ (v) to check that something is happening

3. _____ (v) to keep (someone or something) safe

4. _____ (n) members of the same family

WHILE VIEWING

A ▶ Watch the video. Which of the following are true about the Duke Lemur Center? Check (✓) all that apply.

☐ 1. It has the largest collection of lemurs outside Madagascar.

☐ 2. Only one person works there.

☐ 3. It takes care of lemur babies.

B ▶ Watch the video a second time and answer the questions.

1. Why is it an exciting time at the Duke Lemur Center?
   a. a new species of lemur has been found
   b. some lemur babies have been born

2. How can you check if lemur babies are healthy?
   a. by weighing them
   b. by looking at their eyes

3. What do the babies do during their first 30 days?
   a. learn to climb
   b. eat and sleep

**A mouse lemur at the
Duke Lemur Center**

AFTER VIEWING

A What does Chris Smith mean when he says, "When you look into a lemur's eyes, you can tell that they're looking back"? Note your ideas below. Then discuss with a partner.

_____

B Which animal would you like to help more: lemurs or sea turtles? Why? Complete the sentence below with your own ideas, and then compare with a partner.

I would like to help _____ because _____

_____

Reading 2

PREPARING TO READ

A The words in **blue** below are used in the reading passage on pages 102–105. Match the correct form of each word to its definition. Circle the two words that are antonyms.

BUILDING VOCABULARY

Extinction has long been a part of **nature**. You might be **shocked** to learn that over 90 percent of the species that have ever lived on Earth are now extinct. Scientists think that in the last 600 million years, there have been five mass extinction events. Mass extinctions happen when many species **disappear** in a relatively short time. The last mass extinction happened 65 million years ago, and caused the extinction of the dinosaurs. The **latest** research suggests that, **unfortunately**, we may now be going through a sixth mass extinction—this time caused by human activities. **Fortunately**, many people **care about** animals and are working hard to **save** as many as possible.

1. _____ (n) everything in the world that is not made by people

2. _____ (adv) sadly or unluckily

3. _____ (v) to go away or become unable to be seen

4. _____ (v) to be interested in something and think it is important

5. _____ (v) to keep something away from danger

6. _____ (adj) the most recent

7. _____ (adj) very surprised or upset

8. _____ (adv) happily or luckily

B Note answers to the questions below. Then share your ideas with a partner.

USING VOCABULARY

1. Which animals do you **care about** the most? Why?

_____

2. What animals do you know about that have **disappeared** forever?

_____

C Look at the pictures and read the title and captions on pages 102–105. What is the reading mainly about? Check your idea as you read the passage.

PREDICTING

a. photographs of the world's most endangered animals
b. a photographer who takes pictures to help save endangered species
c. advice on how to take photographs of endangered animals

ANIMALS IN THE FRAME

🎧 12

A Nature photographer Joel Sartore uses his camera to save endangered species. Sartore's photos tell the stories of animals that may disappear unless we work fast to save them.

B Sartore's latest project is called Photo Ark. You can see some photos from the project on pages 103–105. The goal of the project is to make a photographic record of as many animals as possible before they become extinct. As Sartore says, "For many of Earth's creatures, time is running out."[1]

Q How did you become interested in saving endangered species?

A When I was a child, I read about Martha, the very last passenger pigeon. Martha died in 1914. I was shocked. In the past, there were 5 billion passenger pigeons— probably more than any other bird. But here was the last one, and there was no way to save it. How did we let this happen? I couldn't understand it. I still feel the same way. I want to stop this from ever happening again.

Q How does photography help to save endangered species?

A Photography is the best way to show problems to the world. It gets people to care about the problems. It's not enough to just show pretty animals in beautiful places. Now we must show the dangers to these animals as well. The good news is there are many ways to publish[2] stories and photographs on environmental issues. Self-publishing on the Web is one way to do this. Even nonprofessional photographers can help to let people know about these problems.

[1]If you **run out** of something, you have no more of it left.
[2]When you **publish** information, you print it in a book or put it online.

◄ **Martha, believed to be the last passenger pigeon, died in 1914. Only 100 years earlier, these birds were found in large numbers throughout North America.**

▲ A bison poses for a Photo Ark photo. Sartore uses either white or black backgrounds for his photos.

Malayan tiger, Omaha Zoo

Malayan tigers are critically endangered. "We tried photographing him on a big black background," Sartore says, "but he just destroyed it. He looked like he really enjoyed it, too!" Fortunately for Sartore, the tiger didn't have a problem with white paper.

Madagascan fish eagle,
Madagascar

Sartore took this beautiful photo at a zoo in Madagascar. Unfortunately, this eagle is one of the most endangered birds in the world. According to recent studies, the population in the wild is under 100.

The lemur leaf frog is another critically endangered animal. The species was once common in South America, but its population has fallen by 80 percent in the last 10 years. The main causes are disease and loss of habitat.

Lemur leaf frog,
Atlanta Botanical Gardens

Chimpanzee, Lowry Park Zoo

This three-month-old baby chimpanzee is called Ruben. "Ruben's mother left him," says Sartore, "so people at the zoo are raising him. While I took the photo, his caregivers were gently holding him. Baby primates are much like human children—they need a mother to hold on to, even if it's human."

UNDERSTANDING THE READING

UNDERSTANDING
MAIN IDEAS

A Complete the answers to the questions. Then underline the information in the passage that helped you.

1. Why was Sartore shocked when he read about Martha?

   Because _____.

2. Why does Sartore think that photography can help save endangered species?

   Because photography _____.

UNDERSTANDING
DETAILS

B Match each animal from the reading (1–5) with the correct information (a–e).

1. The passenger pigeon _____   a. is named "Ruben."
2. The Madagascan fish eagle _____   b. is extinct.
3. The lemur leaf frog _____   c. has fallen in number by 80 percent.
4. The chimpanzee _____   d. has a population of fewer than 100.
5. The tiger _____   e. tore up Sartore's black paper.

CRITICAL THINKING:
GUESSING MEANING
FROM CONTEXT

C Find and underline the following words in the reading. Use context to identify their meanings. Then complete the definitions.

> **creature** (paragraph B)   **record** (paragraph B)   **issues** (paragraph D)

1. A(n) _____ is a collection of information.
2. A(n) _____ is an important subject or problem.
3. A(n) _____ is a living thing that is not a plant.

CRITICAL THINKING:
EVALUATING

D Note answers to the questions below. Then discuss with a partner.

1. How do the Duke Lemur Center and Joel Sartore help to save endangered species?

Duke Lemur Center	Joel Sartore

2. Which approach do you think is more useful in terms of saving animals?

   I think _____'s approach is more useful because

   _____

   _____

   _____

Writing

EXPLORING WRITTEN ENGLISH

A Read the information below.

LANGUAGE FOR WRITING Giving Reasons

You can use *because* to introduce a reason.

> *Many animals are in danger **because** temperatures around the world are rising.*
> **result**   **reason**

You can use *so* to introduce a result.

> *Joel Sartore takes photos of endangered animals, **so** more people know about them.*
> **reason**   **result**

Notice the comma in the sentence with *so*.

Now read the sentences (1–5). Label each sentence part *reason* or *result*.

1. Fuentes was interested in sea turtles, so she decided to help protect them.

   _____   _____

2. Australia is a good place to study sea turtles because it has a large turtle population.

   _____   _____

3. Fuentes works to protect sea turtles because human activity is endangering them.

   _____   _____

4. Sartore wanted to help endangered species, so he started his Photo Ark project.

   _____   _____

5. It's difficult to see Brazilian porcupines in the wild because they sleep during the day.

   _____   _____

Joel Sartore carefully photographs a caiman.

B Complete the following sentences (1–5). Circle *because* or *so*.

1. The world population is increasing, **because** / **so** there are more cars on the road.
2. I want to help protect the environment, **because** / **so** I take the bus every day.
3. Some sea animals are dying **because** / **so** the ocean is polluted.
4. Sea turtles are critically endangered, **because** / **so** we need to help them.
5. Sartore created Photo Ark **because** / **so** he wanted to help save endangered species.

C Combine the sentences (1–5). Use the words in parentheses.

Example: I care about the environment. I ride a bicycle to work. (because)

  I ride a bicycle to work because I care about the environment.

1. I take the bus to school every day. I want to save money. *(so)*

  _____

2. We recycle plastic. We don't want to pollute the oceans. *(because)*

  _____

3. We want to have cleaner air. Our city planted trees. *(because)*

  _____

4. I turn off the lights when I leave a room. I want to save electricity. *(so)*

  _____

5. We want to save trees. We use both sides of the paper. *(because)*

  _____

EDITING PRACTICE

In sentences with *because* and *so*, remember to:
- use *because* before a reason and *so* before a result.
- use a comma in sentences with *so*.

Find and correct one mistake in each of the sentences.

1. Some animals cannot cope with climate change so we need to help them.

2. Sartore publishes animal photos so he wants to help endangered species.

3. Fuentes wrote a book about sea turtles, so she wanted people to learn about them.

4. The number of male sea turtles is falling so climate change is affecting turtle eggs.

D Read the information below. Then complete the sentences with the present continuous form of the verb in parentheses.

> **LANGUAGE FOR WRITING** Present Continuous Tense
>
> We use the present continuous (*be* + verb-*ing*):
> - to talk about actions happening now.
> - to talk about situations that are changing.
>
>   *People around the world **are working** hard to save endangered animals.*
>   *The sea turtle population **is getting** smaller because people are **hunting** turtles.*
>   *Baby lemurs **are growing** and **getting** healthier in the Duke Lemur Center.*

1. Joel Sartore _____ (*make*) people more aware of endangered species with his photos.

2. The Duke Lemur Center _____ (*help*) to raise baby lemurs.

3. Lemurs are endangered because people _____ (*destroy*) forest habitats.

4. Polar bears _____ (*lose*) their habitats because the polar ice _____ (*melt*).

5. The Florida panther is a critically endangered species. However, conservationists _____ (*work*) hard to protect its forest habitats.

EDITING PRACTICE

In sentences with the present continuous tense, remember to:
- use *be* before an -*ing* verb.
- use the correct form of *be*.
- use an -*ing* verb after *be*.

Correct one mistake in each of the sentences.

1. In some places, sea turtle populations is going up.

2. Sea turtle habitats are in danger because temperatures rising.

3. Mariana Fuentes is help to protect sea turtles.

4. Humans is destroying many animals' habitats.

A critically endangered ▷
Florida panther

WRITING TASK

> **GOAL** You are going to write sentences on the following topic:
> Describe an animal that is in danger. Why is it in danger? What are people doing to help?

PLANNING **A** Choose an endangered animal from this unit that you are interested in. Then make notes about it below.

1. Endangered animal: _____

2. Where does this animal live? _____

3. How many are left in the world? _____

4. Why is it endangered? _____

5. What are people doing to help? _____

FIRST DRAFT **B** Use your notes to write at least five sentences about the animal. Use *because* or *so* and the present continuous tense.

_____

_____

_____

_____

_____

EDITING **C** Now edit your draft. Correct mistakes with *because*, *so*, and the present continuous tense. Use the checklist on page 157.

UNIT REVIEW
Answer the following questions.

1. What two words can you use to introduce a reason?

_____

_____

2. What is one result of climate change?

_____

_____

3. Do you remember the meanings of these words? Check (✓) the ones you know. Look back at the unit and review the ones you don't know.

Reading 1:

☐ cool ☐ effect ☐ fall

☐ in danger ☐ over ☐ rise

☐ safe ☐ temperature ☐ under

☐ warm

Reading 2:

☐ care about ☐ disappear ☐ fortunately

☐ latest ☐ nature ☐ save

☐ shocked ☐ unfortunately

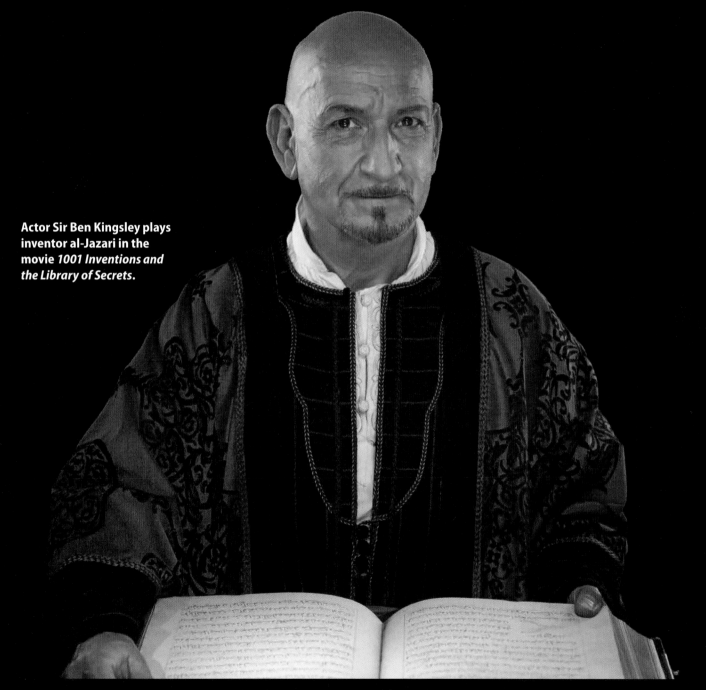

GREAT INVENTORS 7

Actor Sir Ben Kingsley plays
inventor al-Jazari in the
movie *1001 Inventions and
the Library of Secrets*.

ACADEMIC SKILLS

READING	Understanding pronoun reference
WRITING / GRAMMAR	Using simple past tense of *be*
	Using simple past tense of other verbs
CRITICAL THINKING	Analyzing an argument

THINK AND DISCUSS

1 Make a list of items and devices that you
   use every day.
2 Do you know who invented any of the
   things on your list?

A **Look at the information on these pages and answer the questions.**

1. Who developed the first helicopter that flew with a pilot? When?
2. Who completed the first signal flare? When?
3. Who invented the first life raft? When?
4. Which invention do you think was most important? Why?

B **Use the correct form of the words in** yellow **to complete the definitions.**

If you _____ something, you give details about it.

If you _____ something, you are the first person to make it.

A _____ is an object that uses power to move.

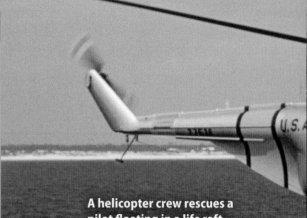

A helicopter crew rescues a pilot floating in a life raft.

A WORLD
OF INVENTIONS

Many people know that Thomas Edison **invented** the lightbulb. However, many inventors of other everyday items are not well known at all. Here are some examples of life-changing inventions with not-so-famous inventors.

Helicopter

The world's first flying machine was described in a fourth-century Chinese book called the *Baopuzi*. It had a spinning design, like today's helicopters. In 1907, Frenchman Paul Cornu built the Cornu Helicopter (pictured). His 20-second flight was the world's first helicopter flight with a pilot.

Signal Flare

In the early 19th century, American Benjamin Franklin Coston started work on the signal flare. After he died in 1848, his wife, Martha Coston, spent 10 years completing the invention. She sold her signal flares to the U.S. government and all over Europe. Since the mid-19th century, signal flares have helped save lives all over the world.

Life Raft

Two inventors—Maria Beasley and Horace Carley—created early designs for a life raft. Beasley created hers in 1882. Carley completed his in 1903. Their designs led to the life rafts found on today's boats and ships.

Reading 1

PREPARING TO READ

A The words in **blue** below are used in the reading passage on pages 115–116. Match the sentence parts to make definitions. Use a dictionary to help you.

1. An **engine** _____   a. works to build or fix things like machines, roads, or bridges.

2. A **drawing** _____   b. is the part of a machine that gives it power.

3. **History** _____   c. is an object that is a copy of something else.

4. A **model** _____   d. refers to events that happened in the past.

5. An **engineer** _____   e. is a picture of something made with a pen or pencil.

B Circle the correct word to complete the definitions.

1. If something **floats** in water, it **will / won't** stay on the top of the water.

2. If something **sinks** in water, it **will / won't** stay on the top of the water.

C List three ideas for each category below. Then share your ideas with a partner.

1. three things that **float** in water

   _____   _____   _____

2. three things that **sink** in water

   _____   _____   _____

3. three things that have an **engine**

   _____   _____   _____

4. three famous people from **history**

   _____   _____   _____

D Read the first paragraph of the reading passage on pages 115–116. What invention does it describe? Why does the author describe the invention as "amazing"? Note your ideas below. Then discuss with a partner.

_____

_____

THE FATHER OF ENGINEERING

🎧 13

Eight hundred years ago, a man in southern Turkey **invented** an amazing clock. It was more than 23 feet (seven meters) high. At its base[1] was a life-size **model** elephant. Every half hour, something amazing happened. The whole clock came alive: Model birds, dragons,[2] and people started to move.

The clock's inventor was an **engineer** named al-Jazari. He lived in Diyarbakir, a city in Turkey. Al-Jazari was probably one of the greatest engineers in **history**. Some historians[3] call him "the father of modern-day engineering."

We know about al-Jazari mostly from a book that he wrote. It **describes** a number of machines of all shapes and sizes. They include clocks, hand-washing machines, and pumps[4] for lifting water. The book also has **drawings** that show how each machine works.

Many everyday items today—from toys to car **engines**—still use al-Jazari's ideas. Without his machines with moving parts, we might not have modern-day robots.

Today, it is still possible to see what al-Jazari's elephant clock looked like. A full-size working model is in Dubai's Ibn Battuta Mall. There, every half hour, al-Jazari's most amazing invention comes to life once again.

[1]The **base** of something is its bottom part.
[2]In stories, a **dragon** is a large animal that looks like a lizard with wings.

[3]A **historian** is a person who studies history.
[4]A **pump** is a machine that makes air or water move in a certain direction.

How Does the Elephant Clock Work?

A bowl with a small hole **floats** in a water tank inside the elephant's body ①. As the bowl slowly **sinks**, it pulls a rope that moves a human figure ②. His moving pen shows the number of minutes past the hour.

Every half hour, the water bowl becomes full and sinks completely. This causes a ball to fall from the top of the clock ③. The movement of the ball causes a phoenix to move and make a sound.

The ball then drops out of a falcon's mouth into the mouth of a Chinese dragon ④. The weight of the ball causes the dragon's head to move down ⑤, and the dragon's tail pulls the water bowl back up.

Finally, the ball drops out of the dragon's mouth and into a vase ⑥. As the ball lands in the vase, the elephant driver moves and makes a sound ⑦. The cycle⁵ begins again until there are no more balls in the top of the clock.

⁵A **cycle** is a series of events that starts again after it has finished.

▷ **In his elephant clock, al-Jazari used ideas from Egypt, China, Greece, and India. The clock was therefore also a celebration of different cultures.**

Phoenix

Falcon

Dragon

Pen

Vase

UNDERSTANDING THE READING

A Complete the summary. Use no more than three words for each blank.

UNDERSTANDING MAIN IDEAS

Al-Jazari was a(n) ¹ _____ who lived in ² _____
around ³ _____ ago. His most famous invention was the
⁴ _____. We know about al-Jazari and his ideas because he
⁵ _____. Many modern-day items or machines use al-Jazari's ideas,
such as a car ⁶ _____.

B How does al-Jazari's elephant clock work? Write the steps (a–e) in the correct sequence in the diagram.

UNDERSTANDING A PROCESS

a. The dragon's tail pulls the bowl back up.
b. After 30 minutes, a ball starts to fall from the top.
c. A bowl floats on the water in the tank.
d. The bowl moves down in the water and pulls on ropes.
e. The ball drops into a dragon's mouth.

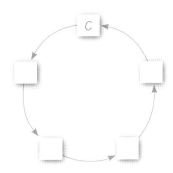

> **CRITICAL THINKING**   **Analyzing** an argument means looking at and understanding a writer's point of view. As you read, ask yourself: *What is the writer's opinion? What evidence does the writer give to support this opinion?*

C Note answers to the questions below. Then discuss with a partner.

CRITICAL THINKING: ANALYZING AN ARGUMENT

1. In paragraph B, what opinion does the author give of al-Jazari?

_____

2. What evidence does the author use to support his/her opinion?

_____

◁ **A full-size working model of the elephant clock in Ibn Battuta Mall, Dubai**

DEVELOPING READING SKILLS

READING SKILL Understanding Pronoun Reference

A pronoun is a word that stands for, or takes the place of, a noun. **Subject pronouns** are *I, he, she, it, you, we,* and *they.* Subject pronouns refer to subjects in sentences. A pronoun usually refers to a noun that comes earlier—in the same sentence or in a previous sentence.

To understand which noun a pronoun refers to, ask yourself these questions:

- Is the pronoun singular (e.g., *he, she, it*) or plural (e.g., *they*)? The pronoun should match the earlier noun.
- Is the pronoun feminine (*she*), masculine (*he*), or gender-neutral (*it, they*)? The gender of the pronoun should match the gender of an earlier noun.

In the example below, the singular masculine pronoun ***he*** refers to the man **al-Jazari**. The plural gender-neutral pronoun ***they*** refers to the plural noun **machines**.

*A man named **al-Jazari** was one of the greatest inventors in history. **He** invented amazing **machines**. **They** were both beautiful and useful.*

UNDERSTANDING
PRONOUNS

A Look at the **bold** pronouns in the paragraph below. Ask these questions about each pronoun:

- Is it singular or plural?
- Is it feminine, masculine, or gender-neutral?

> We know about al-Jazari mostly from a book that **he** wrote. **It** describes a number of machines of all shapes and sizes. **They** include clocks, hand-washing machines, and pumps for lifting water. The book also has drawings that show how each machine works.

UNDERSTANDING
PRONOUNS

B In the paragraph above, draw an arrow to the noun that each pronoun refers to.

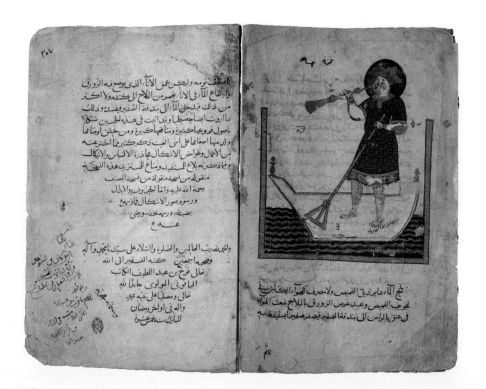

▶ **Pages from al-Jazari's *Book of Knowledge* show one of his water-raising machines.**

Video

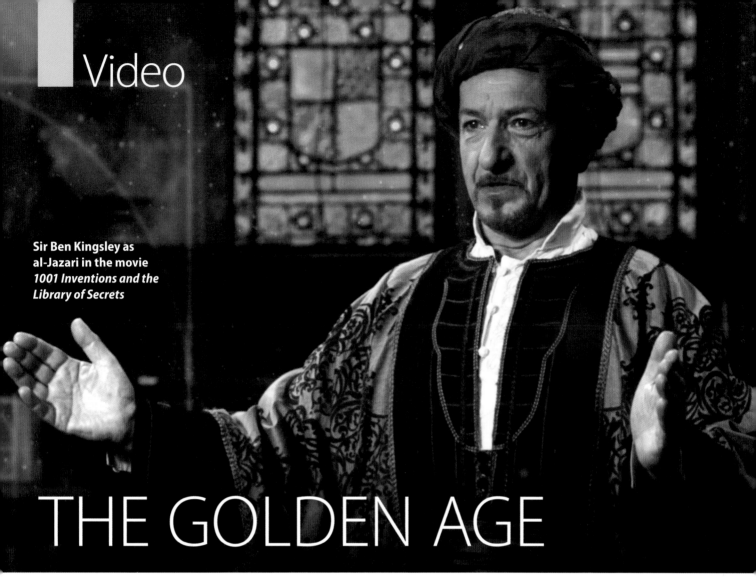

Sir Ben Kingsley as
al-Jazari in the movie
*1001 Inventions and the
Library of Secrets*

THE GOLDEN AGE

BEFORE VIEWING

A Look at the title of the video. The phrase *Golden Age* is used to talk about times in history when people achieved great things. What period in your country's history could be described as a Golden Age? Discuss with a partner.

DISCUSSION

B The words below are used in the video. Match each word with the correct definition.

VOCABULARY IN CONTEXT

The elephant clock was an **ingenious** invention.
Al-Jazari's ideas helped lay the **foundations** of modern engineering.
Al-Jazari's work has had a big **impact** on today's technology.
Ancient Egypt is an example of a very old **civilization**.

1. _____ (n) a strong effect

2. _____ (n) the ideas that other things are based on

3. _____ (adj) new and very clever

4. _____ (n) a group of people with their own society and culture

C Read the information about the Dark Ages. Then answer the questions.

As the Roman Empire spread through Europe, it brought with it many improvements in art and culture. However, after the Roman Empire fell in around A.D. 500, many of these improvements were lost. This period, which lasted hundreds of years, became known as the Dark Ages. Modern historians, however, prefer not to use the term Dark Ages anymore. Research has shown that many great achievements were made in this period, both in Europe and in other parts of the world.

1. Why is the period after A.D. 500 known as the Dark Ages?

_____

2. Why do some historians think that the name is not suitable?

_____

WHILE VIEWING

A ▶ Watch the video. What are two reasons why the librarian believes the Dark Ages should be known as "the Golden Ages"?

☐ a. There were many great discoveries made during this time.

☐ b. Many great artists and writers were born during the period.

☐ c. Ideas from many different cultures around the world came together.

B ▶ Watch the video a second time. Match the sentence parts to make true sentences.

1. Ibn al-Haytham _____   a. made discoveries about engineering.

2. Abbas ibn Firnas _____   b. had early ideas about flying.

3. Al-Jazari _____   c. explained how our eyes work.

AFTER VIEWING

A What modern technology may have benefited from the work of the inventors below? Use information from the video and the reading passage on pages 115–116.

1. Ibn al-Haytham: _____

2. Abbas ibn Firnas: _____

3. Al-Jazari: _____

B Which of the people in activity **A** do you think made the most useful discoveries? Why? Discuss with a partner.

Reading 2

PREPARING TO READ

A The words in blue below are from the reading passage on pages 122–123. Match the correct form of each word to its definition.

BUILDING VOCABULARY

Bill Gates is sometimes called "the father of home computing." Born in 1955, Gates **grew up** in the United States. When he was 13, his school bought one of the earliest computers, and Gates showed **huge** interest in it. After **discussing** it with his teachers, he was allowed to miss math class and instead spend time on the computer. His **aim** was to be able to write his own computer **programs**. Gates became not just a **brilliant** computer programmer but also a smart businessman. In 1975, before he finished university, Gates co-founded Microsoft. As the company became successful, Gates had no **reason** to finish his university studies. In 2015, the company **celebrated** its 40th birthday and is now the world's largest computer software company.

◄ **Bill Gates**

1. _____ (n) a goal; something you want to achieve

2. _____ (n) a statement that explains "why"

3. _____ (adj) very smart

4. _____ (v) to do something special for an important event

5. _____ (v) to become an adult

6. _____ (adj) very big

7. _____ (n) a set of instructions that tell a computer what to do

8. _____ (v) to talk about something

B List three ideas for each category below. Then share your ideas with a partner.

USING VOCABULARY

1. three things you **celebrate** every year

_____ _____ _____

2. three **reasons** to study English

_____ _____ _____

3. three **brilliant** scientists

_____ _____ _____

C Skim the reading on pages 122–123. Who is the reading about? What was her great achievement? Check your ideas as you read the passage.

SKIMMING

THE MOTHER OF COMPUTING

🎧 14

A On October 16 every year, people celebrate Ada Lovelace Day. But who is Ada Lovelace, and what is she famous for?

B When people think of the history of computers, they usually think of men such as Bill Gates and Steve Jobs. These men had a huge effect on the world of computing. But many historians believe the world's first computer programmer was a woman: Lady Augusta Ada King, also known as Ada Lovelace.

C Ada Lovelace was born in 1815 and grew up in London, England. Her mother was a mathematician[1] and, as a young girl, Lovelace was brilliant at math and science. At the age of 13, she even created a design for a flying machine.

D When she was 17 years old, Lovelace met a mathematician named Charles Babbage. They became friends and enjoyed discussing math together. At the time, Babbage was working on a design for a machine called an "Analytical Engine." The machine would be able to work on difficult math problems. Lovelace was very interested.

E In 1843, Lovelace helped write an article on the Analytical Engine. She added her own ideas and notes to it. One of her notes described a step-by-step calculation[2] that the Analytical Engine could perform. Today, the Analytical Engine is thought to be the first design of what we now call a computer. And Lovelace's step-by-step calculation is thought to be the first ever computer program.

F Ada Lovelace was one of very few female mathematicians and scientists in her time. Today, more women and girls study math and science than ever before, but they are still a minority.[3] One reason may be that the most famous mathematicians and scientists are men. The aim of Ada Lovelace Day is to celebrate the achievements of women in science, engineering, and mathematics. In this way, Ada Lovelace continues to be a role model[4] for young women around the world.

[1] A mathematician is someone who studies math.
[2] You make a calculation when you find out a number using math.
[3] A minority of people or things is fewer than half of them.
[4] A role model is a person who inspires others.

▲ A painting of Ada Lovelace in
Whitechapel Art Gallery, London

UNDERSTANDING THE READING

A Why has Ada Lovelace become a role model?

    a. She is an example of someone who never gave up during difficult times.

    b. She came from a poor family but became a brilliant mathematician.

    c. She is a woman who made a great achievement in science and mathematics.

COMPLETING A
SUMMARY

B Complete the summary with information from the reading on pages 122–123.

Ada Lovelace lived during the ¹_____ century. Her mother was a
²_____. When Lovelace was ³_____ years old, she
met a man named ⁴_____. He was designing a machine that could
do ⁵_____ problems. Lovelace was very interested. In 1843, Lovelace
helped to write an article about the machine. She added her own ideas and notes.
The machine is considered one of the first designs of a ⁶_____, and
Lovelace's notes are thought to be the first ever ⁷_____. People who
want the world to remember Lovelace created a day to celebrate her. Ada Lovelace Day
is on ⁸_____ every year.

CRITICAL THINKING:
ANALYZING AN
ARGUMENT

C Note answers to the questions below. Then discuss with a partner.

1. In paragraph C, what adjective does the author use to describe Lovelace's math and
science ability?

_____

2. In the final sentence of the reading passage, what phrase does the author use to
describe his/her opinion of Ada Lovelace?

_____

3. In paragraph E, what evidence does the author give to support his/her opinion?

_____

_____

CRITICAL THINKING:
SYNTHESIZING

D What are three things that al-Jazari and Ada Lovelace have in common? Write your
ideas below. Then discuss with a partner.

_____

_____

_____

Writing

EXPLORING WRITTEN ENGLISH

A Read the information in the box.

> **LANGUAGE FOR WRITING** Simple Past Tense
>
> Use the simple past to talk about completed actions in the past.
>
> _Ada Lovelace_ **lived** _in London, England._
>
> Add _-ed_ to the base form of a regular verb to form the simple past.
>
> invent—invent**ed**
>
> Add _-d_ if the verb already ends in _-e_.
>
> live—live**d**   translate—translate**d**
>
> Make spelling changes for some verbs.
>
> For verbs that end in consonant + _-y_, drop the _-y_ and add _-ied_:
>
> try—tr**ied**   study—stud**ied**   carry—carr**ied**
>
> For most verbs that end in consonant + vowel + consonant, double the final consonant and add _-ed_.
>
> stop—stop**ped**   excel—excel**led**   rob—rob**bed**
>
> Some verbs have irregular past forms.
>
> | | | | |
> |---|---|---|---|
> | become—became | build—built | come—came | eat—ate |
> | find—found | go—went | grow—grew | have—had |
> | make—made | meet—met | put—put | say—said |
>
> For negative statements, use _did not (didn't)_ + the base form of a verb.
>
> _She_ **didn't invent** _the Analytical Engine._

Now write the simple past form of each verb below.

Base Form	Simple Past Form
create	
try	
say	
have	
design	
save	

Base Form	Simple Past Form
begin	
invent	
build	
grow up	
go	
discover	

B Complete the paragraphs with the simple past form of each verb in parentheses.

1. Hungarian László Bíró _____ (*invent*) the first ballpoint pen in the early 20th century. Bíró's brother _____ (*help*) him with the invention. Bíró and his brother were born in Hungary, but they _____ (*go*) to Argentina in 1943. Bíró _____ (*die*) in 1985.

2. In 1903, inventor Mary Anderson _____ (*have*) an idea. She noticed that car drivers _____ (*need*) to open their windows when it rained so that they _____ (*can*) see. Anderson _____ (*create*) a swinging rubber arm that drivers could control by using a lever inside a car. The invention was very popular and _____ (*become*) known as the windshield wiper.

3. Archaeologists _____ (*find*) the world's first bars of soap in Babylon, in modern-day Iraq. Babylonians_____ (*mix*) animal fat with wood ashes and water to make the soap.

C Look at the reading on pages 122–123 to answer the questions. Write complete sentences. Use the simple past.

1. When did Ada Lovelace live?

   _____

2. Where did she grow up?

   _____

3. What did her mother do?

   _____

4. What did she create when she was 13?

   _____

5. Who did she meet when she was 17?

   _____

   _____

6. When did she write the first ever computer program?

   _____

   _____.

**A portrait of Ada Lovelace,
by Alfred Edward Chalon**

D Read the information below. Then complete each sentence (1–8) with the correct simple past form of *be*.

> **LANGUAGE FOR WRITING** Simple Past of *Be*
>
> Use the simple past of *be* to describe people, things, and situations in the past. The verb *be* is usually followed by a noun, an adjective, or a prepositional phrase.
>
> *Ada Lovelace **was** a mathematician.*
> *She **was** talented.*
> *Lovelace and Babbage **were** in London when they met.*
>
> The past forms of *be* are *was/was not* and *were/were not*. You can use contractions for the negative forms: *wasn't* and *weren't*. We usually use contractions when we speak. We do not often use contractions in academic writing.
>
> *Ada Lovelace **was not** a university professor.*
> *There **were not** many female mathematicians in Lovelace's time.*

1. Ada Lovelace _____ good at math.

2. She and Charles Babbage _____ friends.

3. Charles Babbage _____ a mathematician.

4. There _____ many female scientists in Lovelace's time.

5. Lovelace's mother _____ a computer programmer.

6. Al-Jazari _____ an engineer.

7. Al-Jazari and Ada Lovelace _____ doctors.

8. Al-Jazari's elephant clock _____ small.

E Write true sentences (1–4) about famous people in the past. Use the past tense of *be*. Write two affirmative sentences and two negative sentences.

1. _____

2. _____

3. _____

4. _____

WRITING TASK

GOAL You are going to write sentences on the following topic:
Explain why we should have a day to celebrate a particular inventor.

PLANNING **A** Choose an inventor you know about. Make notes in the chart below.

Inventor's Name	What did he/she achieve? Why should we celebrate them?

FIRST DRAFT **B** Use your notes to write five sentences about the inventor. Use the simple past.

Main idea	I think we should celebrate _____.
Where / When was this person born?	He / She was born _____.
Main reason to celebrate this person	We should celebrate him / her because _____ _____ _____.
A second reason	Also, _____ _____.
What should people do on this day?	On this day, people should _____ _____ _____.

EDITING **C** Now edit your draft. Correct mistakes with the simple past. Use the checklist on page 157.

UNIT REVIEW

Answer the following questions.

1. What are the simple past forms of these verbs?

   live _____   try _____   stop _____

   go _____   meet _____   build _____

2. What are some examples of modern day technology that use al-Jazari's ideas?

   _____

   _____

3. Do you remember the meanings of these words? Check (✓) the ones you know. Look back at the unit and review the ones you don't know.

   Reading 1:
   ☐ describe   ☐ drawing   ☐ engine
   ☐ engineer   ☐ float   ☐ history
   ☐ invent   ☐ machine   ☐ model
   ☐ sink

   Reading 2:
   ☐ aim   ☐ brilliant   ☐ celebrate
   ☐ discuss   ☐ grow up   ☐ huge
   ☐ program   ☐ reason

ALIEN WORLDS 8

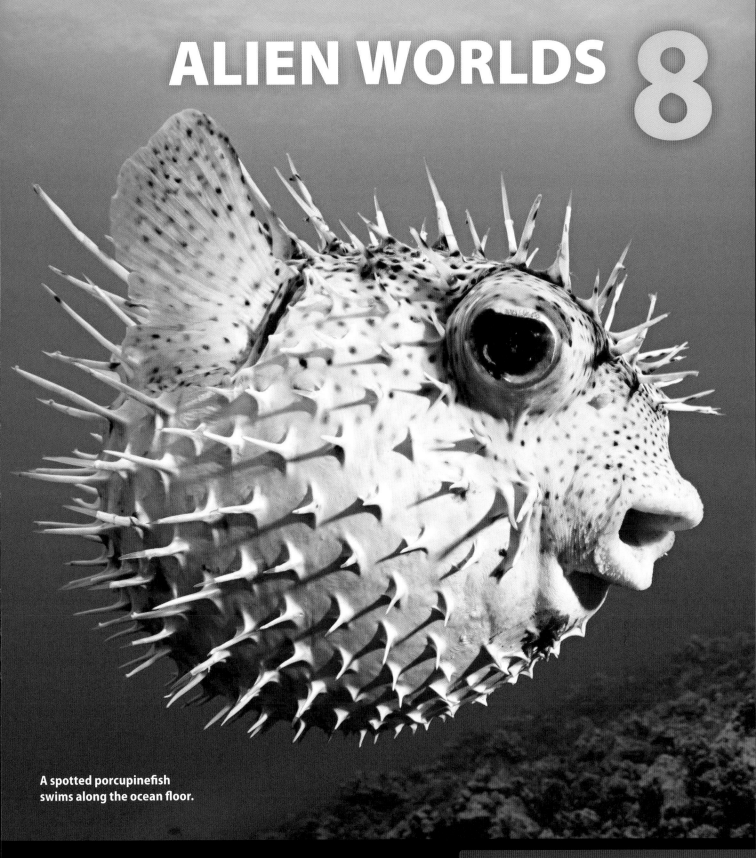

A spotted porcupinefish swims along the ocean floor.

THINK AND DISCUSS

1 Which do you think is more interesting—the ocean or space? Why?

2 Do you think it's more useful to explore the ocean or space? Why?

A Look at the information on these pages and answer the questions.

1. What is the Milky Way? What do we know about it?
2. In which part of the Milky Way do we live?
3. What does the Milky Way look like when seen from Earth?

B Use the correct form of the words in blue to complete the sentences.

Our _____ is called Earth.

Earth has just a _____ moon, while Jupiter has 67.

The sun is a _____.

0°

10,000

SCUTUM ARM

20,000

P E R S E U S   A R M

S A G I T T A R I U S

60°

30,000

90°

40,000

50,000 light-years

Direction of rotation

120°

O U T E R

150°

OUR HOME IN SPACE

The Milky Way Galaxy—our home—has hundreds of billions of **stars**. Our solar system—which includes the sun, Earth, Mars, Venus, and other **planets**—is in a part of the galaxy called the Orion Arm. The solar system may seem big to us, but it is a small part of our galaxy. Light from one end of the galaxy would take 100,000 years to travel to the other side. However, the Milky Way is just a **single** galaxy, and it is small compared to the universe. Astronomers—scientists who study space—think there are billions of galaxies beyond our Milky Way.

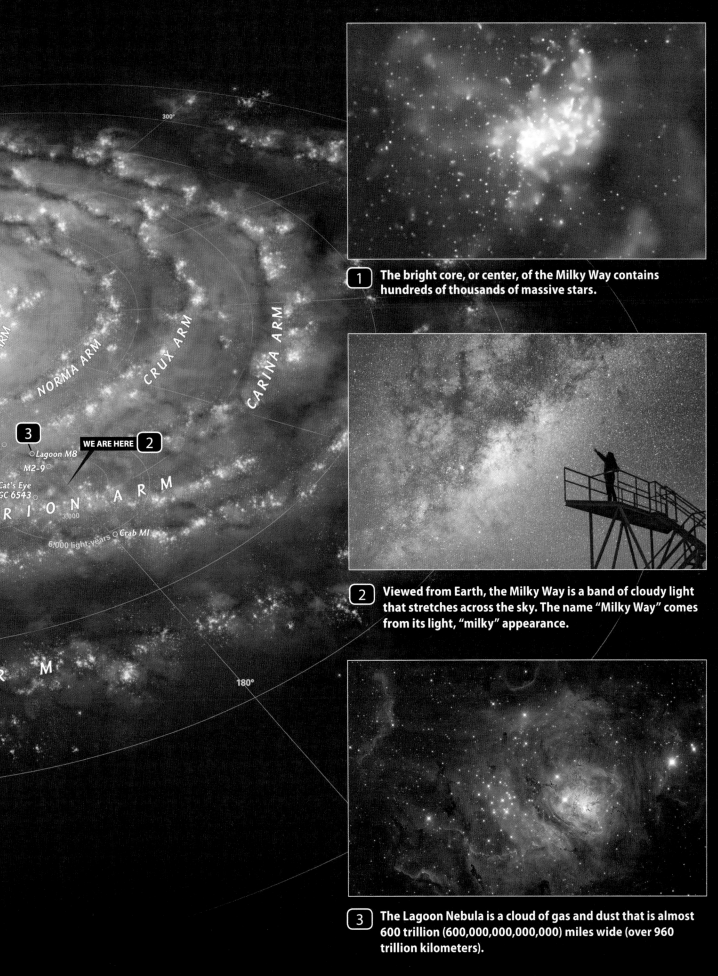

300°

ARM

NORMA ARM

CRUX ARM

CARINA ARM

3 ○

○ Lagoon M8

M2-9 ○

Cat's Eye
GC 6543 ○

WE ARE HERE **2**

R I O N A R M

3,000

6,000 light-years ○ Crab MI

180°

R M

M

R

1 The bright core, or center, of the Milky Way contains hundreds of thousands of massive stars.

2 Viewed from Earth, the Milky Way is a band of cloudy light that stretches across the sky. The name "Milky Way" comes from its light, "milky" appearance.

3 The Lagoon Nebula is a cloud of gas and dust that is almost 600 trillion (600,000,000,000,000) miles wide (over 960 trillion kilometers).

Reading 1

PREPARING TO READ

BUILDING
VOCABULARY

A The words in blue below are used in the reading passage on pages 133–134. Match the correct form of each word with its definition.

> At a **distance** of around 60 million kilometers, Mercury is the **nearest** planet to the sun.
>
> Scientists believe that in the past, conditions on Mars may have been **suitable** for **life**.
>
> It takes around eight minutes for light from the sun to **reach** Earth.
>
> Astronomers **discovered** the dwarf planet Pluto in 1930.
>
> Scientists are **excited** by the fact that there is an ocean of water beneath the surface of Saturn's moon Enceladus.

1. _____ (v) to find something for the first time

2. _____ (v) to arrive at

3. _____ (adj) very interested and happy

4. _____ (adj) right for something

5. _____ (adj) close, not far

6. _____ (n) the amount of space between two things

7. _____ (n) things that are alive

USING
VOCABULARY

B Answer the questions below with a partner. Use the diagram at the bottom of the page to help.

1. Which **planet** is the biggest in the solar system?

2. Which is **nearer** the sun: Mars or Venus?

3. Why do you think conditions on Pluto are not **suitable** for **life**?

PREVIEWING

C Read the first paragraph of the reading on pages 133–134. What two questions does the author ask? What do you think the answers to these questions are? Discuss your ideas with a partner.

The Solar System

Mercury   Earth   Jupiter   Saturn   Uranus   Neptune

Venus   Mars

Plu

An artist's idea of the surface of an exoplanet in the Trappist-1 star system

OTHER WORLDS

🎧 15

A   Look up at the sky on a dark, moonless night. There are many thousands of **stars**. But are there other **planets** like Earth? And could humans live there one day?

B   New technology is helping astronomers **discover** hundreds of new planets. So far, we know of more than 3,500 "exoplanets." These are planets that move around stars other than the sun. Some exoplanets may be similar to Earth.

C   An Earthlike exoplanet must have certain features.[1] It needs to be the right **distance** from its star. It will then have a **suitable** temperature for living things: not too cold and not too hot. A planet at the right distance from its star might also have water. Where there is water, there might also be **life**.

D   Recent discoveries have shown that Earthlike exoplanets may be more common than once thought. In 2016, scientists were **excited** to find seven Earthlike exoplanets around a **single** star—Trappist-1. Each planet is a similar size to Earth, and each may have water. Although the seven planets are all very close to the star, Trappist-1 is much cooler than our sun. Temperatures could therefore be suitable for life.

[1] A **feature** of something is an interesting or important part of it.

In the future, a starship like this might carry thousands of people to a new home planet.

Could it be possible for humans to live on an Earthlike planet one day? The biggest problem is distance. The **nearest** star system, Alpha Centauri, is 4.3 light-years[2] from Earth. In 2016, scientists found an Earthlike exoplanet in this system. However, traveling there with today's technology would take thousands of years.

With future technology, however, this may change. Scientist Andreas Tziolas thinks that one day we might be able to travel to another star system. He thinks that new technology will let us **reach** the nearest star in a few decades.[3] "I believe we can achieve some form of interstellar[4] exploration within a hundred years," he says.

[2] A **light-year** is the distance that light travels in one year. It equals about 9.46 trillion (9,460,000,000,000) kilometers.
[3] A **decade** is 10 years.
[4] If something is **interstellar**, it occurs between two or more stars.

UNDERSTANDING THE READING

A Match each of these main ideas with a paragraph (B–F) from the reading.

UNDERSTANDING MAIN IDEAS

_____ 1. Traveling to exoplanets is difficult because they are very far away.

_____ 2. Exoplanets that are similar to Earth might have water and maybe even life.

_____ 3. Astronomers have found many exoplanets.

_____ 4. Scientists found seven Earthlike exoplanets around the same star.

_____ 5. In the future, new technology may allow humans to travel to an exoplanet.

B Answer the questions. Circle the correct option.

UNDERSTANDING DETAILS

1. What is an exoplanet?
   a. a planet that is similar in size to Earth
   b. a planet that moves around a star outside our solar system

2. According to the passage, what is true about Alpha Centauri?
   a. It is the closest star system to Earth.
   b. It has more Earthlike exoplanets than any other star system.

3. What does Andreas Tziolas believe?
   a. We already have the technology to travel to Alpha Centauri.
   b. Travel to another star system will be possible in the future.

C Complete the notes about the Trappist-1 star system.

UNDERSTANDING DETAILS

The Trappist-1 star and its seven exoplanets

- The system contains seven exoplanets that are a similar size to [1]_____.
- The planets are very [2]_____ to the star, but Trappist-1 is very [3]_____ compared to other stars.
- The planets may have [4]_____ and therefore possibly life.

> **CRITICAL THINKING** **Speculation** involves making a guess or prediction. It is important to identify which parts of an article are speculation and which are facts.

D Read the following sentences from the article. Check (✓) the sentences that are speculation. Circle the words that helped you decide.

CRITICAL THINKING: IDENTIFYING SPECULATION

☐ 1. New technology is helping astronomers discover hundreds of new planets.
☐ 2. Earthlike exoplanets may be more common than once thought.
☐ 3. Trappist-1 is much cooler than our sun.
☐ 4. Temperatures could therefore be suitable for life.
☐ 5. One day we might be able to travel to another star system.

DEVELOPING READING SKILLS

READING SKILLS Taking Notes

Taking notes as you read can help you remember important information in a passage. It will also help you remember key ideas for a writing task or test.

As you read, note key nouns, such as names, places, and times. Include details about each one. Also, note how ideas and information relate to each other. For example, note any causes and effects, problems and solutions, steps in a process, or events in a story. Remember that when you write notes, you don't need to write complete sentences.

It can be helpful to note information using an outline or a graphic organizer. Here is one example:

Outline

Main Idea
    Detail
    Detail

Main Idea
    Detail
    Detail

TAKING NOTES **A** Complete the outline using information from pages 133–134.

p. 133 para B
- **Main Idea:** astronomers use new _____ to find exoplanets
- **Detail:** so far, found more than _____
- **Detail:** some may be like _____

p. 134 para E
- **Main Idea:** main problem with traveling to an exoplanet is _____
- **Detail:** nearest star system is _____ away
- **Detail:** traveling there would take _____ years

APPLYING **B** Now create your own outline for paragraph F on page 134.

- **Main Idea:**

- **Detail:**

- **Detail:**

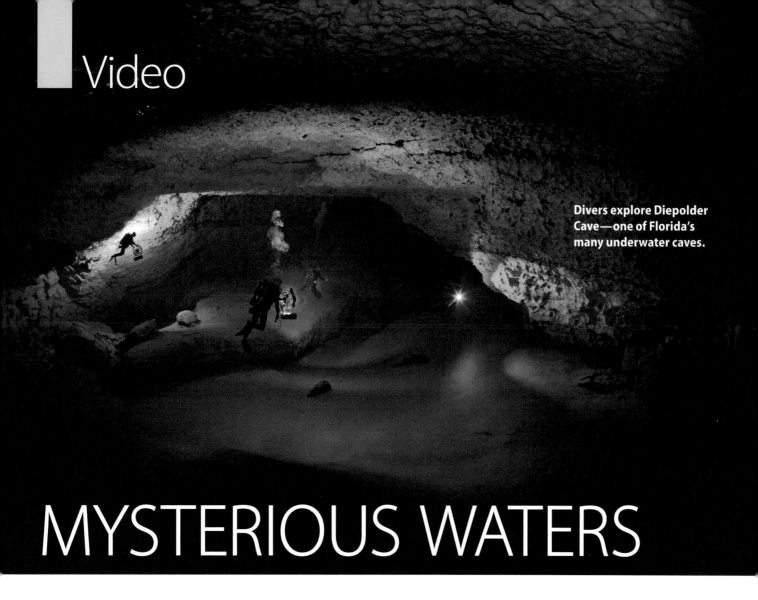

Video

Divers explore Diepolder Cave—one of Florida's many underwater caves.

MYSTERIOUS WATERS

BEFORE VIEWING

A Look at the photo and read the caption. Where are the people? What do you think they can learn from exploring a place like this? Discuss your ideas with a partner.

DISCUSSION

B The words in **bold** below are used in the video. Match the correct form of each word to its definition.

VOCABULARY IN CONTEXT

An echo is created when sound **bounces** off a surface and returns to the listener.

It's hard to swim in water that has a strong **current** because it can push you in the wrong direction.

An underwater cave system can be like a **labyrinth**. It is very easy to get lost.

A **three-dimensional** (3D) map of a city shows how tall the buildings are.

1. _____ (adj) not flat, having a shape

2. _____ (n) water moving in one direction

3. _____ (n) a place in which it's difficult to find your way, like a maze

4. _____ (v) to hit a surface and then quickly move away from it

C **Read the information about the Wakulla Springs cave system. Then answer the questions.**

Florida's Wakulla Springs is one of the largest underwater cave systems in the world. When it was first explored in 1955, explorers found the bones of land animals that lived thousands of years ago. They also found a number of items that belonged to humans. The explorers realized that a long time ago, the area was above sea level. As the caves filled with water, the animal bones and other objects were kept safe for thousands of years.

1. What two things did divers find when the caves were first explored?

   _____

2. What did this tell the explorers about the area?

   _____

WHILE VIEWING

UNDERSTANDING
MAIN IDEAS

A ▶ **Watch the video. What was the purpose of the team's dive?**

   a. to look for the bones of ancient animals

   b. to study animal species living in the caves

   c. to create a map of the caves

UNDERSTANDING
DETAILS

B ▶ **Watch the video a second time and complete the notes.**

- Diving can be very [1]_____: Around [2]_____ divers have died in Florida's caves since 1960.

- Boyd Matson makes a mistake: kicks up a lot of [3]_____ and can't see. Uses a [4]_____ to get out.

- Divers use a machine to [5]_____ sound waves off the cave walls to create a 3D map.

- Deep in the cave, the [6]_____ is very strong. But in the end, the divers return safely to the surface. The dive is successful.

AFTER VIEWING

REACTING TO THE
VIDEO

A Would you like to explore underwater caves? Why or why not? Note your ideas below. Then discuss with a partner.

   _____

   _____

CRITICAL THINKING:
SYNTHESIZING

B How are the challenges of exploring underwater similar to the challenges of exploring space? Note your ideas below. Then discuss with a partner.

   _____

   _____

   _____

Reading 2

PREPARING TO READ

A The words in blue below are used in the reading passage on pages 140–141. Complete the definitions using the correct form of the words.

reading passage on pages 140–141

BUILDING VOCABULARY

> Most of space is a **mystery** to us. We don't know much about it.
> A layer of gray dust **covers** the moon.
> You have to use a special **vehicle** to explore **deep** parts of the ocean.

1. _____ (n) something that you cannot explain or understand
2. _____ (n) a machine that moves people or things from one place to another
3. _____ (v) to make a layer over the top of something
4. _____ (adj) far below the surface of something

B Read the definitions below. Then complete each sentence with the correct word.

BUILDING VOCABULARY

> A **variety** is a number of different kinds or examples of something.
> An **illness** is a disease, or a period of being sick.
> If you **complete** a task or a journey, you finish it.
> The **beginning** of something is the first part of it.

1. There are a _____ of reasons that people decide to study space.

2. In 1840, the British explorer Sir James Clark Ross used a tool to get samples from the ocean floor. Some believe this was the _____ of deep-sea exploration.

3. You should not go swimming if you have an _____ like a cold or the flu.

4. In 22 years, the space shuttle Columbia _____ 27 flights into space.

C List three ideas for each category below. Then share your ideas with a partner.

USING VOCABULARY

1. three animals that live **deep** in the ocean

   _____ _____ _____

2. three **vehicles** that are used in water

   _____ _____ _____

3. three common **illnesses**

   _____ _____ _____

D You are going to read an article about deep-sea exploration. Why do you think it might be useful to explore the deepest parts of the oceans? Work with a partner and list some ideas. Then read the passage to see which of your ideas are mentioned.

PREDICTING

A   Oceans have always seemed mysterious. In the past, people believed that giant dragons and other monsters lived deep in the seas. Other people imagined mermaids[1] and underwater cities.

B   Today, much of the world's oceans are still a mystery. "The oceans cover 71 percent of our planet," says oceanography[2] professor Dr. Robert Ballard. "Yet only 5 percent of it has been explored." In fact, we know more about some areas of Mars than about some parts of the world's oceans.

MOUNTAINS IN THE SEA

C   New technology, however, is helping scientists explore these hidden worlds. For example, scientists are using an underwater vehicle called DeepSee to explore seamounts—underwater mountains.

D   Scientists have used DeepSee to study Las Gemelas, an area of seamounts near Costa Rica. A huge variety of species lives on and around Las Gemelas. Some of these species have never been seen before. Some may have chemicals that can help people fight illnesses, such as cancer.

DOWN IN THE DEPTHS

E   The deepest place on Earth is the Mariana Trench in the Pacific Ocean. The ocean floor there is about 36,000 feet (11,000 meters) deep. In 2012, filmmaker and explorer James Cameron reached the Mariana Trench in a vehicle called Deepsea Challenger. He was the first person to complete the journey alone. Cameron took photos and video on the ocean floor. He also collected underwater samples.[3]

F   Vehicles such as Deepsea Challenger are helping us discover new animals and plants. Some of these have been around for millions of years. These discoveries could help us better understand how life on our planet began. Deep-sea exploration also helps us in other ways. For example, we are learning how underwater earthquakes cause tsunamis.[4] As Cameron says, "This is the beginning of opening up [a] new frontier."[5]

[1]In stories, a **mermaid** is a woman with a fish's tail who lives in the ocean.
[2]**Oceanography** is the study of the ocean.
[3]A **sample** is a small amount of something that shows you what the rest is like.
[4]A **tsunami** is a very large wave that can cause damage on land.
[5]A **frontier** is a place that people are just starting to explore.

Some strange creatures live in the deepest parts of the oceans, such as the frilled shark (top), viperfish (middle), and giant spider crab (bottom).

The underwater vehicle DeepSee explores a seamount in Las Gemelas.

UNDERSTANDING THE READING

UNDERSTANDING THE GIST

A Which of the following would be the best alternative title for the reading?

a. Deep-Sea Discoveries   b. Saving Sea Creatures   c. Underwater Earthquakes

UNDERSTANDING DETAILS

B Complete the notes about the reading passage.

(Paras A and B) Oceans = mystery

cover _____ of Earth

expl'd _____

we know more about _____

(Paras C and D) New tech. → explore more

vehicle called _____

went to _____ near _____

(Paras E and F) Deepest place in ocean = _____

2012: _____ explored alone

he took _____ and collected _____

deep-sea exploration helps us understand how _____

also learn about how _____ cause _____

CRITICAL THINKING: GUESSING MEANING FROM CONTEXT

C The words below are synonyms—words with similar meanings—of words in the reading passage. Scan the reading to find the correct synonyms.

1. (Paragraph A) dreamed _____

2. (Paragraph C) unseen _____

3. (Paragraph F) findings _____

CRITICAL THINKING: ANALYZING AN ARGUMENT

D Note answers to the questions below using information from the reading passage.

1. What do ocean scientists and explorers study underwater?

_____

_____

2. Why is their work useful? (What are some possible benefits?)

_____

_____

CRITICAL THINKING: SYNTHESIZING

E Look back at your answer to question 1 on page 129. Has your opinion changed? Complete the sentence and list two reasons. Share your ideas in a small group.

I think _____ exploration is more interesting.

Reason 1: _____

Reason 2: _____

Writing

EXPLORING WRITTEN ENGLISH

A Read the information below.

LANGUAGE FOR WRITING Introducing Your Opinion

You can use the verbs *think* and *believe* to introduce an opinion about something.

> **I think** *we can reach Mars someday.*
> **I don't think** *we can ever reach Mars.*
> **I believe** *we can learn a lot by studying space.*
> **I don't believe** *we can learn much by studying space.*

You can also use the phrase *in my opinion*. Remember to use a comma after *in my opinion*.

> **In my opinion,** *humans will need to move to another planet one day.*
> **In my opinion,** *humans won't be able to live on Earth forever.*

Now complete the sentences (1–6). Use positive or negative forms to give your own opinion. Use the correct forms of the words in parentheses in the last two sentences (5–6).

think / don't think

1. I _____ many humans will live on another planet 50 years from now.

2. I _____ scientists will discover life on Mars.

believe / don't believe

3. I _____ it's important to spend a lot of money on space exploration.

4. I _____ governments should spend more money on exploration than on education.

In my opinion, / In my opinion, . . . not

5. _____, space exploration (*be*) _____ important.

6. _____, astronomers (*have*) _____ a more interesting job than ocean explorers.

NASA's Curiosity rover captured this image from the surface of Mars.

B Write your opinion about each of the ideas below. In each sentence, use a different phrase to introduce your opinion.

Example: *Space exploration can help us learn about our own planet.*
   I believe space exploration can help us learn about our own planet.

1. Studying the ocean is a waste of time and money.

   _____

2. Life forms from other planets are looking for us.

   _____

3. People will live on an exoplanet 100 years from now.

   _____

C Read the information below.

LANGUAGE FOR WRITING Using Modal Verbs to Make Predictions

You can use modals to make predictions about the future. For example, you can use *will* to make predictions you are sure about. Use *may* and *might* to make predictions you are less sure about.

   *Any mission to Mars **will** be very expensive.* (certain)
   *Underwater exploration **may** help us understand how life began.* (less certain)
   *Traveling to another world **might** be possible in the future.* (less certain)

Remember: Use the base form of the verb after a modal verb.

To make a negative statement, add *not* after the modal verb.

   *There **might not** be a mission to Mars before 2050.*

Now unscramble the words and phrases to make sentences.

1. in tall apartment buildings / will / in the future / live / I think / most people /.

   _____

2. be / cities like / New York and Beijing / even more crowded / might /.

   _____

3. apartment buildings / people / leave / might never / their / need to /.

   _____

4. most people / in my / home / opinion, / work / from / will /.

   _____

D Circle the best option to complete each sentence.

1. I **will** / **might** not be able to play soccer this weekend. I'll let you know by Friday.
2. I heard it **will** / **may** snow tomorrow. The weatherman said there's a 50 percent chance.
3. There's no way that we **will** / **might** ever live on Jupiter.
4. I **will** / **may** come to the party, but I haven't decided yet.
5. Next year, my birthday **will** / **might** be on a Tuesday.

EDITING PRACTICE

Read the information. Then find and correct one mistake in each of the sentences.

In sentences with *may, might,* and *will,* remember:
- to use the base form of the verb.
- to use *will* for things you are sure about. Use *may* or *might* when you are not sure.

1. Robots may replaced doctors someday.

2. I think people will having computers inside their bodies in the future.

3. Someday, we might to build homes underground.

4. I believe new telescopes will finding many more exoplanets in the future.

5. We will be able to see Saturn in the sky tonight. It depends if the skies are clear.

Radio telescopes in Chile observe the night sky.

WRITING TASK

GOAL You are going to write sentences on the following topic:

Express your opinion about the future of space or ocean exploration.

PLANNING **A** Make notes in the chart below using information from this unit. Add ideas of your own.

Astronomers study space because . . .	Ocean scientists study the sea because . . .

FIRST DRAFT **B** Use your ideas to answer this question: *What should governments spend more money on—space exploration or ocean exploration?* Use opinion expressions and *will*, *might*, and *may*.

Main idea	_____ governments should spend more money on _____ exploration than _____ exploration.
Reason 1	With _____ exploration, we can learn more about _____.
Reason 2	Also, _____ _____.
Reason 3	Finally, _____ because _____.

EDITING **C** Now edit your draft. Correct mistakes with modal verbs. Use the checklist on page 157.

UNIT REVIEW

Answer the following questions.

1. What are two phrases you can use to introduce your opinion?

_____

2. What can people learn by studying the deepest parts of our oceans?

_____

_____

3. Do you remember the meanings of these words? Check (✓) the ones you know. Look back at the unit and review the ones you don't know.

Reading 1:

☐ discover   ☐ distance   ☐ excited
☐ life   ☐ near   ☐ planet
☐ reach   ☐ single   ☐ star
☐ suitable

Reading 2:

☐ beginning   ☐ complete   ☐ cover
☐ deep   ☐ illness   ☐ mystery
☐ variety   ☐ vehicle AWL

VOCABULARY EXTENSION UNIT 1

WORD FORMS Superlative Adjectives

Use superlative adjectives to compare one idea to other ideas. Follow the rules below.

	ADJECTIVE	SUPERLATIVE
- For most short adjectives add -est	fast	the fastest
- For adjectives ending in -e add -st	large	the largest
- For adjectives ending in -y add -iest	busy	the busiest
- For many longer adjectives use most	expensive	the most expensive
- For adjectives ending in a vowel and then a consonant, double the final consonant	big	the biggest

A Complete each sentence by writing the correct superlative form of the adjective in parentheses.

1. Beijing is a big city, but _____ (big) city in China is Shanghai.

2. The Duge Bridge is _____ (high) bridge in the world.

3. China had one of _____ (early) human societies in the world.

4. The Shanghai Maglev Train is _____ (fast) train in the world.

5. Soccer is popular in China, but _____ (popular) spectator sport is basketball.

WORD WEB Social Media Words

Below are some common words that appear on social media sites.

Your online **profile** often includes your name, photo, and other personal information.
When you **update** your profile, you change or add new information about yourself.
When you **follow** someone online, you choose to get updates from that person.
A **feed** is the information, stories, or photos you get from people you are following.
If an item on your feed is **trending**, it is very popular right now.

B Match the sentence parts.

1. I added a new photo to my _____   a. trending online.

2. I am interested in music, so I _____   b. profile.

3. I get a lot of news items on my _____   c. follow the most popular bands.

4. Right now, a new cat video is _____   d. feed.

5. I will update my profile because _____   e. I just got married.

VOCABULARY EXTENSION   UNIT 2

WORD LINK Synonyms

Synonyms are words that are very similar in meaning. For example the words *large* and *big* are synonyms.

A Match each word with the correct synonym. Use a dictionary to check your answers.

_____ 1. smart   a. little

_____ 2. begin   b. hard

_____ 3. around   c. start

_____ 4. small   d. about

_____ 5. difficult   e. unhappy

_____ 6. sad   f. clever

B Choose two of the words in exercise **A** and write a sentence using each one.

_____

_____

WORD WEB Time Words and Phrases

We use adverbs of time to describe when an event will happen.
Some adverbs of time do not indicate a specific time.

Soon: in a short time

Later: at some time after now

Someday: an unknown time in the future

Some adverbs of time are more specific.

This weekend

Next year

In five/ten years time

C Complete each sentence with your own ideas.

1. Later today, I plan to _____.

2. This weekend, I plan to _____.

3. Next year, I want to _____.

4. In five years' time, I want to _____.

5. Someday, I hope to _____.

VOCABULARY EXTENSION   UNIT 3

Collocations are words that often go together, such as *business trip*. Some collocations are in the noun + noun form. Here are some common collocations with the noun *trip*.

business trip: a trip taken as part of someone's job

road trip: a long trip by car or motorcycle

fishing trip: a trip to go fishing

field trip: a trip to study something

A Complete each sentence with the correct form of the collocations from the box above.

1. Next week, the school students are going on a _____ to the science museum.

2. A sales representative goes on many _____ to see customers far away.

3. I'm going on a _____ this weekend to try and catch some tuna.

4. My friend and I are going on a _____ through Europe next year. We're driving from Paris to Moscow.

WORD WEB Prepositions of Place and Direction

Prepositions of place describe where things are.

*The library is **near** the town hall.*

*I parked my car **between** two buses.*

*They sat **opposite** each other at dinner.*

Prepositions of direction describe how things move. Prepositions of direction usually modify a verb of movement.

*He walked **across** the road.*

*I flew **over** India on my way to Europe.*

*You need to drive **through** a long tunnel to get there.*

B Circle the best preposition to complete each sentence.

1. To get to Manhattan, you can go **through** / **over** the Brooklyn Bridge.

2. The world-famous Times Square is **between** / **through** 42nd and 47th Streets. The Empire State Building is **near** / **across** Times Square.

3. My office is directly **opposite** / **between** the Empire State Building.

4. Many tourists like walking **opposite** / **through** Central Park.

VOCABULARY EXTENSION   UNIT 4

Here are some common verb + noun collocations with the noun *photos*.

edit *a photo*: to fix a photo using a computer (e.g. brightening the image)

download *a photo*: to move a photo from a camera to a computer

upload *a photo*: to move a photo from a computer to a website

share *a photo*: to show a photo to a group of friends online

print *a photo*: to produce a copy of a photo on a machine

A Circle the best word to complete each sentence.

1. During my trip to London, I **printed** / **took** hundreds of photos of the city and **uploaded** / **took** them to my Facebook page.

2. My internet connection was slow, so it took a long time to **print** / **download** the photo.

3. I **share** / **edit** all my photos with my friends online.

4. I **downloaded** / **printed** a photo of my family and put it on my wall.

WORD FORMS Nouns and Verbs with the Same Spelling

Some words can be spelled in the same way as both nouns and verbs. For example, *guess* (the noun) is spelled the same way as *guess* (the verb).

VERB

*Can you **guess** which photo is fake?*

NOUN

My best ***guess*** is this photo is fake.

B Read the sentences below. Write **N** for noun or **V** for verb above each underlined word.

1. A photographer <u>dreams</u> of taking the perfect picture.

2. Taking photos on top of Mount Everest involves a long and difficult <u>climb</u>.

3. It was a silly <u>plan</u> to post a fake photograph online.

4. Many people <u>contact</u> friends using online social media.

5. I use my <u>phone</u> to post photos online.

VOCABULARY EXTENSION   UNIT 5

WORD LINK -ous

Some nouns can be made into adjectives by adding -ous. The suffix -ous means "full of."
For example, *poisonous* means full of poison. Follow these spelling rules:

For most nouns add -ous	poison—poison**ous**
For most nouns ending in -e, cut the -e and add -ous	fame—fam**ous**
For most nouns ending in -y, change the -y to -i and add -ous	mystery—myster**ious**

A Complete each sentence with the adjective form of the nouns below.

> adventure   danger   fame   mountain   vary

1. I am not very _____. I don't like high-risk activities such as skydiving.

2. Daron Rahlves is a(n) _____ skier. He won many races and also appeared in several movies.

3. There are _____ reasons why people take risks. One reason is that taking risks makes people feel good.

4. Most ski resorts are found in _____ areas of the world.

5. Skydiving can be a(n) _____ activity. Some people have died or been seriously hurt.

WORD PARTNERS Nouns/Adjectives + *size*

Here are some common nouns and adjectives that collocate with the word *size*.

average size	**class** size	**shoe** size
actual size	**right** size	**wrong** size

B Complete each sentence with one of the collocations from the box above.

1. As a teacher, my perfect _____ is about eight to ten students.

2. This is only a model. The _____ is three times bigger.

3. This shirt doesn't fit me. It's the _____.

4. Different parts of the world have different systems for measuring _____. For example, a size 11 in the United States is a 10.5 in the United Kingdom.

5. In 2013, the _____ of a new home in the United States was 50% bigger than in 1983.

WORD FORMS Comparative Adjectives

We use comparative adjectives to compare two things. For example:

*A car is **bigger than** a bicycle.*

Follow these spelling rules:

- For most one-syllable adjectives add *-er*. For words that end consonant-vowel-consonant, double the final consonant and add *-er*. For words ending in *-e* just add *-r*.

cool—cool**er**   big—bigg**er**   nice—nice**r**

- For most two-syllable adjectives ending in *-y* replace the *-y* with *-i* and add *-er*.

busy—bus**ier**

- For most two- or three-syllable adjectives add *more*.

expensive—**more** expensive

A Complete each sentence using the comparative form of the adjective in parentheses and *than*.

1. A chimpanzee is _____ (small) an elephant.

2. An elephant is _____ (heavy) a chimpanzee.

3. Surfing is _____ (adventurous) sitting on your couch.

4. Tropical areas of the planet are _____ (warm) polar areas.

5. Photographing animals in a studio is _____ (safe) photographing them in the wild.

WORD PARTNERS Verbs + *about*

We often use the preposition *about* to introduce a topic. It often follows a verb. For example:

*Let's **talk about** the problems you are having at school.*
*I **worry about** global warming. I think it's a big problem.*
*I often **think about** my grandma. I remember how kind she was.*
*We often **laugh about** all the silly things we did as kids.*
*For my next essay, I will **write about** endangered animals.*
*I **care about** what happens to the blue-throated macaw.*

B Circle the best collocation to complete each sentence.

1. Many people **laugh** / **worry** about global warming. They think it could have a bad effect on the planet.

2. In a recent article, *National Geographic Magazine* **wrote** / **thought** about the effects of global warming.

3. I saw my teacher after class and we **talked** / **cared** about my poor grade.

4. Most teachers **write** / **care** about their students. They want their students to do well.

5. Joel Sartore takes photos of endangered species to make people **laugh** / **care** more about them.

VOCABULARY EXTENSION   UNIT 7

WORD FORMS Changing Verbs to Nouns with *-ing*

Some verbs can be turned into nouns by adding *-ing*. The suffix *-ing* indicates the result of the verb form. For example *a drawing* is the result of the action to *draw*.

A Complete each sentence with the correct forms of the words below. Include *a* or *an* if necessary.

| build | end | meet | paint | record |

1. Journalists often _____ interviews on their smartphones. They use these _____ to write their reports.

2. The worlds tallest _____ is in Dubai. It was _____ in 2008.

3. Leonardo de Vinci _____ the *Mona Lisa*—one of the most famous _____ in the world.

4. For most teenagers, school _____ when they are 18 years old.

5. The team _____ every week to discuss the project. The _____ usually lasts one hour.

WORD LINK Occupation Words with *-er* or *-or*

Some nouns that end with *-er* or *-or* refer to "a person that does a job." For example, an *author* is someone who writes books.

B Complete each sentence with the best word from the box. Add *a* or *an*.

| engineer | explorer | inventor | photographer | teacher |

1. Someone who travels to new places is _____.

2. _____ uses a camera.

3. Someone who works to build bridges is _____.

4. _____ works in a school.

5. Someone who creates new things is _____.

VOCABULARY EXTENSION   UNIT 8

Some adjectives begin with *un-*. The prefix *un-* means "not" and indicates an opposite meaning. For example, if something is *unsuitable*, it means it is not *suitable*.

A Circle the best word to complete each sentence.
1. Scientists are now **certain / uncertain** there are planets moving around stars in other parts of the universe. Many exoplanets have been found using powerful telescopes.
2. The universe is so big. I find it **surprising / unsurprising** that there are some Earthlike exoplanets.
3. The surface temperature of Mercury can reach 800°F. The conditions are **suitable / unsuitable** for life.

B Circle an adjective and complete each sentence with your own opinion.
1. I think it is **likely / unlikely** that humans will live on another planet because _____
   _____ .
2. I think living on another planet would be **pleasant / unpleasant** because _____
   _____ .

Some adjectives can be made into nouns by adding *-ness*. The suffix *-ness* means the quality or state of something. For example, an *illness* is the state of being ill. For adjectives ending in *-y*, change the *-y* to an *-i* and add *-ness* (happy—happ**iness**).

C Complete each sentence using the noun form of the words below.

dark	fit	happy	ill	kind	sad

1. There was _____ today at the news that giant panda Jia Jia died after suffering from a short _____ .
2. _____ is important for professional soccer players. Some soccer players run more than 10 kilometers every game.
3. My grandmother was known for her _____ . For example, she made food for her neighbors and looked after their children.
4. A lot of people believe that money alone doesn't bring _____ .
5. During the night, the house was in complete _____ .

Independent Student Handbook

TIPS FOR READING FLUENTLY

Reading slowly, one word at a time, makes it difficult to get an overall sense of the meaning of a text. As a result, reading becomes more challenging and less interesting. In general, it is a good idea to first skim a text for the gist, and then read it again more closely so that you can focus on the most relevant details. Use these strategies to improve your reading speed:

- Read groups of words rather than individual words.
- Keep your eyes moving forward. Read through to the end of each sentence or paragraph instead of going back to reread words or phrases.
- Skip functional words (articles, prepositions, etc.) and focus on words and phrases carrying meaning—the content words.
- Use clues in the text—such as **bold** words and words in *italics*—to help you know which parts might be important and worth focusing on.
- Use section headings, as well as the first and last lines of paragraphs, to help you understand how the text is organized.
- Use context clues, affixes and parts of speech—instead of a dictionary—to guess the meaning of unfamiliar words and phrases.

TIPS FOR READING CRITICALLY

As you read, ask yourself questions about what the writer is saying, and how and why the writer is presenting the information at hand.

Important critical thinking skills for academic reading and writing:

- **Analyzing:** Examining a text in detail to identify key points, similarities, and differences.
- **Applying:** Deciding how ideas or information might be relevant in a different context.
- **Evaluating:** Using evidence to decide how relevant, important, or useful something is.
- **Inferring:** "Reading between the lines"; in other words, identifying what a writer is saying indirectly, or implicitly, rather than directly, or explicitly.
- **Synthesizing:** Gathering appropriate information and ideas from more than one source and making a judgment, summary, or conclusion based on the evidence.
- **Reflecting:** Relating ideas and information in a text to your own personal experience.

TIPS FOR NOTE TAKING

Taking notes will help you better understand the overall meaning and organization of a text. Note taking also helps you to record the most important information for future uses—such as when you have a writing assignment. Use these techniques to improve your note taking:

- As you read, highlight important information such as dates, names, places, and other facts.
- Take notes in the margin. Note the main idea and supporting details next to each paragraph. Also note your own ideas or questions about the paragraph.
- On a separate piece of paper, write notes about the key points of the text in your own words. Include short headings, key words, page numbers, and quotations.
- Keep your notes brief by using abbreviations Stnd symbols.

TIPS FOR LEARNING VOCABULARY

You often need to use a word or phrase several times before it enters your long-term memory. Here are some strategies for successfully learning vocabulary:

- Use flash cards to test your knowledge of new vocabulary. Write the word you want to learn on one side of an index card. Write the definition and/or an example sentence that uses the word on the other side.

- Use a vocabulary journal to note down a new word or phrase. Write a short definition of the word in English and the sentence where you found it. Write another sentence of your own that uses the word. Include any common collocations (see *Word Partners* in the Vocabulary Extensions).

- Make word webs or word maps. See below for an example.

- Use memory aids to remember a word or phrase. For example, if you want to learn the idiom *keep an eye on someone*, which means "to watch someone carefully," you might picture yourself putting your eyeball on someone's shoulder so that you can watch the person carefully. The stranger the picture is, the more likely you will remember it!

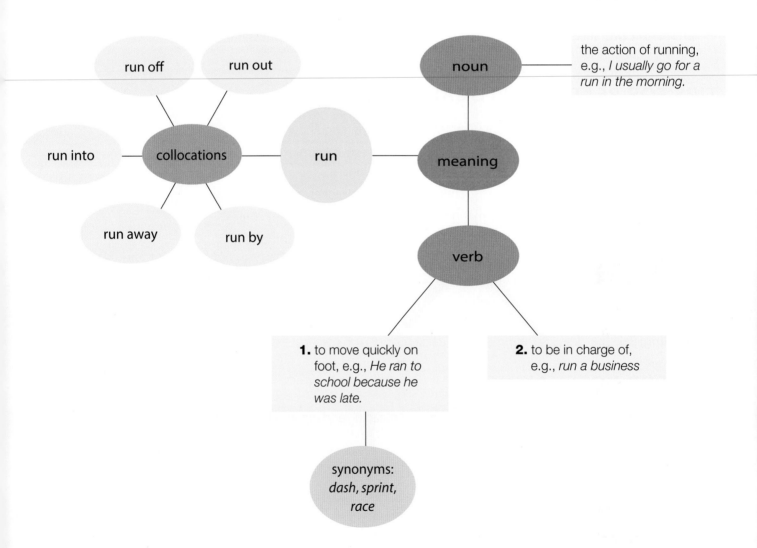

TIPS FOR EDITING

Capitalization

Remember to capitalize:

- the first letter of the word at the beginning of every sentence.
- proper nouns such as names of people, places, companies, movies, and books.
- days, months, and holidays.
- the word *I*.
- the words in titles that have meaning (content words). Don't capitalize *a, an, the, and*, or prepositions such as *to, for, of, from, at, in,* and *on,* unless they are the first word of a title (e.g., *Hooked on Adventure*).

Punctuation

- Use a period (.) at the end of any sentence that is not a question.
- Exclamation marks (!), which indicate strong feelings such as surprise or joy, are generally not used in academic writing.
- Use commas (,) to separate a list of three or more things. (*She speaks German, English, and Spanish.*)
- Use a comma after an introductory word or phrase. (*In my opinion, people will live on Mars in fifty years.*)
- Use a comma before a combining word—and, but, so, or—that joins two sentences. (*Skydiving looks like fun, but it's too risky for me.*)
- Use an apostrophe (') for showing possession. (*Brian Skerry's job is sometimes dangerous.*)
- Use quotation marks (" ") to indicate the exact words used by someone else. (*As Cameron says, "This is the beginning of opening up a new frontier."*)

EDITING CHECKLIST

Use the checklist to find errors in your writing task for each unit.

	Unit							
	1	2	3	4	5	6	7	8
1. Is the first word of every sentence capitalized?								
2. Does every sentence end with the correct punctuation?								
3. Does every sentence contain a subject and a verb?								
4. Do your subjects and verbs agree?								
5. Do all possessive nouns have an apostrophe?								
6. Are all proper nouns capitalized?								
7. Is the spelling of places, people, and other proper nouns correct?								

UNIT 1
Language for Writing: Simple Present Tense of *Be* and Other Verbs

Be				Other verbs	
I	am ('m)		I You We They	play soccer. go swimming. have English class.
You We They	are ('re)	happy. sad. here.			
He She It	is ('s)	at work.	He She It	plays soccer. goes swimming. has English class.

UNIT 5
Language for Writing: Simple Present Tense (Negative)

Be				Other verbs	
I	am not ('m not)		I You We They	do not (don't)	like tennis.
You We They	are not (aren't / 're not)	happy. sad. here.			
He She It	is not (isn't / 's not)	at work.	He She It	does not (doesn't)	

UNIT 5
Language for Writing: Adverbs of Frequency

Be				Other verbs	
I	am ('m)	always usually often sometimes hardly ever never	busy.	I You We They He She It	always usually often sometimes hardly ever never	eat(s) breakfast.
You We They	are ('re)				
He She It	is ('s)				

UNIT 6
Language for Writing: Present Continuous Tense

Affirmative			Negative		
I	am ('m)		I	am not ('m not)	
You We They	are ('re)	listening.	You We They	are not (aren't / 're not)	listening.
He She It	is ('s)		He She It	is not (isn't / 's not)	

UNIT 7
Language for Writing: Simple Past Tense of *Be* and Other Verbs

Be			Other verbs		
I He She It	was	happy. sad. here. at work.	I You We They He She It	played soccer. went to the store. had lunch.	
	was not (wasn't)				
You We They	were			didn't	have lunch play soccer. go to the store.
	were not (weren't)				

UNIT 8
Language for Writing: Modal Verbs for Predictions

Affirmative			Negative		
I You We They He She It	will ('ll) might may	be late. arrive soon.	I You We They He She It	will not (won't) might not may not	be on time. arrive until later.

Note: Use *will* for things that are certain. Use *might* or *may* for things that are uncertain.

VOCABULARY INDEX

Word	Unit	CEFR Level	Word	Unit	CEFR Level
achieve*	2	B1	drawing	7	A1
across	3	A2	dream (n)	2	A2
activity	5	A2	earn	2	A2
add	1	A2	effect	6	B1
adventure	3	A2	engine	7	A2
afraid	5	A2	engineer	7	A2
aim (v)	7	B1	enjoy	5	A1
amazing	3	A2	excited	8	A1
anywhere	3	A2	expensive	2	A1
appear	4	B1	fall	6	A2
around	1	A2	find out	4	A2
available*	1	A2	float	7	B1
begin	2	A1	follow	5	A2
beginning	8	A1	fortunately	6	B1
believe	4	A2	goal*	5	A2
brain	5	A2	grow	1	A2
brilliant	7	A2	grow up	7	A2
business	5	A1	guess (v)	4	A2
capital	3	A2	hiking	3	-
care about	6	A2	history	7	A2
celebrate	7	B1	hobby	4	A2
check out	3	B1	hotel	1	A1
choose	3	A1	however	1	A2
city	1	A1	huge	7	B1
click on	4	A2	idea	2	A2
climb	3	A2	illness	8	B1
close (adj)	5	A1	important	3	A1
communicate*	4	B1	in danger	6	A2
company	2	A2	interested in	2	A2
complete	8	A2	invent	7	B1
contact*	4	A2	job*	1	A1
cool	6	A2	join	4	A2
country	1	A1	large	1	A2
countryside	1	A2	latest	6	A2
cover (v)	8	A2	life	8	A1
crowd	3	A2	location*	3	B1
dangerous	5	A2	low-cost	3	A2
deep	8	A2	machine	7	A2
describe	7	A2	map	3	A2
different	1	A1	missing	4	A2
difficulty	5	B1	model	7	A2
direction	4	B1	museum	3	A1
disappear	6	B1	mystery	8	B1
discover	8	B1	nature	6	A2
discuss	7	A2	near	8	A1
distance	8	B1	nearby	3	B1

Word	Unit	CEFR Level	Word	Unit	CEFR Level
news	1	A2	soon	2	A1
opinion	4	B1	star	8	A2
over	6	A2	strong	5	A2
perhaps	2	A2	succeed	5	B1
photo	4	A1	suitable	8	B1
plan (v)	2	A2	surprisingly	5	B1
planet	8	B1	temperature	6	A2
pleasant	5	A2	together	2	A1
popular	1	A2	tour (n)	3	A2
possible	2	A1	travel	2	A1
post	4	A2	trip	3	A2
practice	2	A2	trouble	5	B1
prize	4	A2	under	6	A1
program (n)	7	A2	unfortunately	6	A2
reach	8	B1	user	4	B1
real	4	A2	variety	8	A2
reason	7	A2	vehicle*	8	B1
restaurant	1	A1	visit	1	A1
return	2	A2	warm	6	A1
rise	6	B1	without	5	A2
safe	6	A1	world	1	A1
save	6	A2			
shadow	4	B1			
shocked	6	B1			
show (n)	2	A2			
single	8	A2			
sink (v)	7	A2			
site*	1	A2			
situation	5	B1			
size	5	A2			
smart	2	B1			

*These words are on the Academic Word List (AWL). The AWL is a list of the 570 most frequent word families in academic texts. It does not include the most frequent 2,000 words of English.

ACKNOWLEDGMENTS

The Authors and Publisher would like to acknowledge the teachers around the world who participated in the development of the second edition of *Pathways*.

A special thanks to our Advisory Board for their valuable input during the development of this series.

ADVISORY BOARD

Mahmoud Al Hosni, Modern College of Business and Science, Oman; **Safaa Al-Salim**, Kuwait University; **Laila Al-Qadhi**, Kuwait University; **Julie Bird**, RMIT University Vietnam; **Elizabeth Bowles**, Virginia Tech Language and Culture Institute, Blacksburg, VA; **Rachel Bricker**, Arizona State University, Tempe, AZ; **James Broadbridge**, J.F. Oberlin University, Tokyo; **Marina Broeder**, Mission College, Santa Clara, CA; **Shawn Campbell**, Hangzhou High School; **Trevor Carty**, James Cook University, Singapore; **Jindarat De Vleeschauwer**, Chiang Mai University; **Wai-Si El Hassan**, Prince Mohammad Bin Fahd University, Saudi Arabia; **Jennifer Farnell**, University of Bridgeport, Bridgeport, CT; **Rasha Gazzaz**, King Abdulaziz University, Saudi Arabia; **Keith Graziadei**, Santa Monica College, Santa Monica, CA; **Janet Harclerode**, Santa Monica Community College, Santa Monica, CA; **Anna Hasper**, TeacherTrain, UAE; **Phoebe Kamel Yacob Hindi**, Abu Dhabi Vocational Education and Training Institute, UAE; **Kuel-plng Hsu**, National Tsing Hua University; **Greg Jewell**, Drexel University, Philadelphia, PA; **Adisra Katib**, Chulalongkorn University Language Institute, Bangkok; **Wayne Kennedy**, LaGuardia Community College, Long Island City, NY; **Beth Koo**, Central Piedmont Community College, Charlotte, NC; **Denise Kray**, Bridge School, Denver, CO; **Chantal Kruger**, ILA Vietnam; **William P. Kyzner**, Fuyang AP Center; **Becky Lawrence**, Massachusetts International Academy, Marlborough, MA; **Deborah McGraw**, Syracuse University, NY; **Mary Moore**, University of Puerto Rico; **Raymond Purdy**, ELS Language Centers, Princeton, NJ; **Anouchka Rachelson**, Miami Dade College, Miami, FL; **Fathimah Razman**, Universiti Utara Malaysia; **Phil Rice**, University of Delaware ELI, Newark, DE; **Scott Rousseau**, American University of Sharjah, UAE; **Verna Santos-Nafrada**, King Saud University, Saudi Arabia; **Eugene Sidwell**, American Intercon Institute, Phnom Penh; **Gemma Thorp**, Monash University English Language Centre, Australia; **Matt Thurston**, University of Central Lancashire, UK; **Christine Tierney**, Houston Community College, Houston, TX; **Jet Robredillo Tonogbanua**, FPT University, Hanoi.

GLOBAL REVIEWERS

ASIA

Antonia Cavcic, Asia University, Tokyo; **Soyhan Egitim**, Tokyo University of Science; **Caroline Handley**, Asia University, Tokyo; **Patrizia Hayashi**, Meikai University, Urayasu; **Greg Holloway**, University of Kitakyushu; **Anne C. Ihata**, Musashino University, Tokyo; **Kathryn Mabe**, Asia University, Tokyo; **Frederick Navarro Bacala**, Yokohama City University; **Tyson Rode**, Meikai University, Urayasu; **Scott Shelton-Strong**, Asia University, Tokyo; **Brooks Slaybaugh**, Yokohama City University; **Susanto Sugiharto**, Sutomo Senior High School, Medan; **Andrew Zitzmann**, University of Kitakyushu.

LATIN AMERICA AND THE CARIBBEAN

Raul Bilini, ProLingua, Dominican Republic; **Alejandro Garcia**, Colegio Marcelina, Mexico; **Humberto Guevara**, Tec de Monterrey, Campus Monterrey, Mexico; **Romina Olga Planas**, Centro Cultural Paraguayo Americano, Paraguay; **Carlos Rico-Troncoso**, Pontificia Universidad Javeriana, Colombia; **Ialê Schetty**, Enjoy English, Brazil; **Aline Simoes**, Way To Go Private English, Brazil; **Paulo Cezar Lira Torres**, APenglish, Brazil; **Rosa Enilda Vasquez**, Swisher Dominicana, Dominican Republic; **Terry Whitty**, LDN Language School, Brazil.

MIDDLE EAST AND NORTH AFRICA

Susan Daniels, Kuwait University, Kuwait; **Mahmoud Mohammadi Khomeini**, Sokhane Ashna Language School, Iran; **Müge Lenbet**, Koç University, Turkey; **Robert Anthony Lowman**, Prince Mohammad bin Fahd University, Saudi Arabia; **Simon Mackay**, Prince Mohammad bin Fahd University, Saudi Arabia.

USA AND CANADA

Frank Abbot, Houston Community College, Houston, TX; **Hossein Aksari**, Bilingual Education Institute and Houston Community College, Houston, TX; **Sudie Allen-Henn**, North Seattle College, Seattle, WA; **Sharon Allie**, Santa Monica Community College, Santa Monica, CA; **Jerry Archer**, Oregon State University, Corvallis, OR; **Nicole Ashton**, Central Piedmont Community College, Charlotte, NC; **Barbara Barrett**, University of Miami, Coral Gables, FL; **Maria Bazan-Myrick**, Houston Community College, Houston, TX; **Rebecca Beal**, Colleges of Marin, Kentfield, CA; **Marlene Beck**, Eastern Michigan University, Ypsilanti, MI; **Michelle Bell**, University of Southern California, Los Angeles, CA; **Linda Bolet**, Houston Community College, Houston, TX; **Jenna Bollinger**, Eastern Michigan University, Ypsilanti, MI; **Monica Boney**, Houston Community College, Houston, TX; **Nanette Bouvier**, Rutgers University – Newark, Newark, NJ; **Nancy Boyer**, Golden West College, Huntington Beach, CA; **Lia Brenneman**, University of Florida English Language Institute, Gainesville, FL; **Colleen Brice**, Grand Valley State University, Allendale, MI; **Kristen Brown**, Massachusetts International Academy, Marlborough, MA; **Philip Brown**, Houston Community College, Houston, TX; **Dongmei Cao**, San Jose City College, San Jose, CA; **Molly Cheney**, University of Washington, Seattle, WA; **Emily Clark**, The University of Kansas, Lawrence, KS; **Luke Coffelt**, International English Center, Boulder, CO; **William C. Cole-French**, MCPHS University,

Boston, MA; **Charles Colson**, English Language Institute at Sam Houston State University, Huntsville, TX; **Lucy Condon**, Bilingual Education Institute, Houston, TX; **Janice Crouch**, Internexus Indiana, Indianapolis, IN; **Charlene Dandrow**, Virginia Tech Language and Culture Institute, Blacksburg, VA; **Loretta Davis**, Coastline Community College, Westminster, CA; **Marta Dmytrenko-Ahrabian**, Wayne State University, Detroit, MI; **Bonnie Duhart**, Houston Community College, Houston, TX; **Karen Eichhorn**, International English Center, Boulder, CO; **Tracey Ellis**, Santa Monica Community College, Santa Monica, CA; **Jennifer Evans**, University of Washington, Seattle, WA; **Marla Ewart**, Bilingual Education Institute, Houston, TX; **Rhoda Fagerland**, St. Cloud State University, St. Cloud, MN; **Kelly Montijo Fink**, Kirkwood Community College, Cedar Rapids, IA; **Celeste Flowers**, University of Central Arkansas, Conway, AR; **Kurtis Foster**, Missouri State University, Springfield, MO; **Rachel Garcia**, Bilingual Education Institute, Houston, TX; **Thomas Germain**, University of Colorado Boulder, Boulder, CO; **Claire Gimble**, Virginia International University, Fairfax, VA; **Marilyn Glazer-Weisner**, Middlesex Community College, Lowell, MA; **Amber Goodall**, South Piedmont Community College, Charlotte, NC; **Katya Goussakova**, Seminole State College of Florida, Sanford, FL; **Jane Granado**, Texas State University, San Marcos, TX; **Therea Hampton**, Mercer County Community College, West Windsor Township, NJ; **Jane Hanson**, University of Nebraska – Lincoln, Lincoln, NE; **Lauren Heather**, University of Texas at San Antonio, San Antonio, TX; **Jannette Hermina**, Saginaw Valley State University, Saginaw, MI; **Gail Hernandez**, College of Staten Island, Staten Island, NY; **Beverly Hobbs**, Clark University, Worcester, MA; **Kristin Homuth**, Language Center International, Southfield, MI; **Tim Hooker**, Campbellsville University, Campbellsville, KY; **Raylene Houck**, Idaho State University, Pocatello, ID; **Karen L. Howling**, University of Bridgeport, Bridgeport, CT; **Sharon Jaffe**, Santa Monica Community College, Santa Monica, CA; **Andrea Kahn**, Santa Monica Community College, Santa Monica, CA; **Eden Bradshaw Kaiser**, Massachusetts International Academy, Marlborough, MA; **Mandy Kama**, Georgetown University, Washington, D.C.; **Andrea Kaminski**, University of Michigan – Dearborn, Dearborn, MI; **Eileen Kramer**, Boston University CELOP, Brookline, MA; **Rachel Lachance**, University of New Hampshire, Durham, NH; **Janet Langon**, Glendale Community College, Glendale, CA; **Frances Le Grand**, University of Houston, Houston, TX; **Esther Lee**, California State University, Fullerton, CA; **Helen S. Mays Lefal**, American Learning Institute, Dallas, TX; **Oranit Limmaneeprasert**, American River College, Sacramento, CA; **Dhammika Liyanage**, Bilingual Education Institute, Houston, TX; **Emily Lodmer**, Santa Monica Community College, Santa Monica, CA; **Ari Lopez**, American Learning Institute, Dallas, TX; **Nichole Lukas**, University of Dayton, Dayton, OH; **Undarmaa Maamuujav**, California State University, Los Angeles, CA; **Diane Mahin**, University of Miami, Coral Gables, FL; **Melanie Majeski**, Naugatuck Valley Community College, Waterbury, CT; **Judy Marasco**, Santa Monica Community College, Santa Monica, CA; **Murray McMahan**, University of Alberta, Edmonton, AB, Canada; **Deirdre McMurtry**, University of Nebraska Omaha, Omaha, NE; **Suzanne Meyer**, University of Pittsburgh, Pittsburgh, PA; **Cynthia Miller**, Richland College, Dallas, TX; **Sara Miller**, Houston Community College, Houston, TX; **Gwendolyn Miraglia**, Houston Community College, Houston, TX; **Katie Mitchell**, International English Center, Boulder, CO; **Ruth Williams Moore**, University of Colorado Boulder, Boulder, CO; **Kathy Najafi**, Houston Community College, Houston, TX; **Sandra Navarro**, Glendale Community College, Glendale, CA; **Stephanie Ngom**, Boston University, Boston MA, **Barbara Niemczyk**, University of Bridgeport, Bridgeport, CT; **Melody Nightingale**, Santa Monica Community College, Santa Monica, CA; **Alissa Olgun**, California Language Academy, Los Angeles, CA; **Kimberly Oliver**, Austin Community College, Austin, TX; **Steven Olson**, International English Center, Boulder, CO; **Fernanda Ortiz**, University of Arizona, Tucson, AZ; **Joel Ozretich**, University of Washington, Seattle, WA; **Erin Pak**, Schoolcraft College, Livonia, MI; **Geri Pappas**, University of Michigan – Dearborn, Dearborn, MI; **Eleanor Paterson**, Erie Community College, Buffalo, NY; **Sumeeta Patnaik**, Marshall University, Huntington, WV; **Mary Peacock**, Richland College, Dallas, TX; **Kathryn Porter**, University of Houston, Houston, TX; **Eileen Prince**, Prince Language Associates, Newton Highlands, MA; **Marina Ramirez**, Houston Community College, Houston, TX; **Laura Ramm**, Michigan State University, East Lansing, MI; **Chi Rehg**, University of South Florida, Tampa, FL; **Cyndy Reimer**, Douglas College, New Westminster, BC, Canada; **Sydney Rice**, Imperial Valley College, Imperial, CA; **Lynnette Robson**, Mercer University, Macon, GA; **Helen E. Roland**, Miami Dade College, Miami, FL; **Maria Paula Carreira Rolim**, Southeast Missouri State University, Cape Girardeau, MO; **Jill Rolston-Yates**, Texas State University, San Marcos, TX; **David Ross**, Houston Community College, Houston, TX; **Rachel Scheiner**, Seattle Central College, Seattle, WA; **John Schmidt**, Texas Intensive English Program, Austin, TX; **Mariah Schueman**, University of Miami, Coral Gables, FL; **Erika Shadburne**, Austin Community College, Austin, TX; **Mahdi Shamsi**, Houston Community College, Houston, TX; **Osha Sky**, Highline College, Des Moines, WA; **William Slade**, University of Texas, Austin, TX; **Takako Smith**, University of Nebraska – Lincoln, Lincoln, NE; **Barbara Smith-Palinkas**, Hillsborough Community College, Tampa, FL; **Paula Snyder**, University of Missouri, Columbia, MO; **Mary Evelyn Sorrell**, Bilingual Education Institute, Houston, TX; **Kristen Stauffer**, International English Center, Boulder, CO; **Christina Stefanik**, The Language Company, Toledo, OH; **Cory Stewart**, University of Houston, Houston, TX; **Laurie Stusser-McNeill**, Highline College, Des Moines, WA; **Tom Sugawara**, University of Washington, Seattle, WA; **Sara Sulko**, University of Missouri, Columbia, MO; **Mark Sullivan**, University of Colorado Boulder, Boulder, CO; **Olivia Szabo**, Boston University, Boston, MA; **Amber Tallent**, University of Nebraska Omaha, Omaha, NE; **Amy Tate**, Rice University, Houston, TX; **Aya C. Tiacoh**, Bilingual Education Institute, Houston, TX; **Troy Tucker**, Florida SouthWestern State College, Fort Myers, FL; **Anne Tyoan**, Savannah College of Art and Design, Savannah, GA; **Michael Vallee**, International English Center, Boulder, CO; **Andrea Vasquez**, University of Southern Maine, Portland, ME; **Jose Vasquez**, University of Texas Rio Grande Valley, Edinburg, TX; **Maureen Vendeville**, Savannah Technical College, Savannah, GA; **Melissa Vervinck**, Oakland University, Rochester, MI; **Adriana Villarreal**, Universidad Nacional Autonoma de Mexico, San Antonio, TX; **Summer Webb**, International English Center, Boulder, CO; **Mercedes Wilson-Everett**, Houston Community College, Houston, TX; **Lora Yasen**, Tokyo International University of America, Salem, OR; **Dennis Yommer**, Youngstown State University, Youngstown, OH; **Melojeane (Jolene) Zawilinski**, University of Michigan – Flint, Flint, MI.

CREDITS

Photos

Cover, iii © Leyla Emektar, **iv** (tl) AP/ David Guttenfelder/National Geographic Creative, **iv** (cl) NASA Photo/Alamy Stock Photo, **iv** (cl) © Juan Pablo de Miguel Moreno/Aurora Photos, **iv** (bl) Jordan Pix/Getty Images, **vi** (tl) © Corey Rich/Aurora Photos, **vi** (cl) Joel Sartore, National Geographic Photo Ark/National Geographic Creative, **vi** (cl) 1001 Inventions Ltd, **vi** (bl) © Design Pics Inc./National Geographic Creative, **1** (c) AP/David Guttenfelder/National Geographic Creative, **2–3** (c) Cengage Learning, Inc., **5** (t) Fritz Hoffmann/National Geographic, **6** (bl) Prof. Stan Z. Li and his research team of the Center for Biometrics and Security Research, **6** (br) Prof. Stan Z. Li and his research team of the Center for Biometrics and Security Research, **9** (tc) © NASA, **12–13** (c) Cengage Learning, Inc., **15** (b) Design Pics Inc./National Geographic Creative, **19** (c) NASA Photo/Alamy Stock Photo, **20–21** (c) Cengage Learning, Inc., **22** (b) kamilpetran/Shutterstock, **24–25** (c) Jon Ross/National Geographic Creative, **27** (t) © Robbie Shone/National Geographic Creative, **29** (tr) Paul Kane/Getty Images, **30** (br) © Emily Ainsworth, **31** (c) Emily Ainsworth, **37** (c) © Juan Pablo de Miguel Moreno/Aurora Photos, **38–39** (c) Malgorzata Brewczyk/Alamy Stock Photo, **41** (t) © Alastair Humphreys, **42** (c) © Alastair Humphreys, **45** (t) © Alastair Humphreys, **48** (br) Peter Phipp/Travelshots.com/Alamy Stock Photo, **48–49** (c) © Cengage Learning, Inc., **49** (tl) David M. Benett/Getty Images, **50** (bc) Tim M/Alamy Stock Photo, **51** (bc) © Sergio Pitamitz/National Geographic Creative, **52** (bc) Robert Harding Picture Library/National Geographic Creative, **55** (c) Jordan Pix/Getty Images, **56** (bc) Science & Society Picture Library/Getty Images, **56** (bl) Apic/Getty Images, **56** (br) Royal Photographic Society/Getty Images, **57** (tl) Andreas Feininger/Getty Images, **57** (bc) For Alan/Alamy Stock Photo, **57** (tc) Adrian Lyon/Alamy Stock Photo, **59** (t) © Chris Burkard/Massif, **60** (bc) © Chris Burkard/Massif, **63** (t) Frans Lanting/National Geographic Creative, **64** (bc) Brian J. Skerry/National Geographic Creative, **67** (t) © Alexyz3d/Shutterstock, **67** (bc) © Chris Fallows, **73** (c) © Corey Rich/Aurora Photos, **74–75** (c) © Mauricio Graiki/Shutterstock, **77** (t) Adam Pretty/Getty Images, **78** (b) Bloomberg/Getty Images, **81** (t) © Brady Barr/National Geographic Creative, **82** (br) © Joel Sartore/National Geographic Creative, **84** (c) ZUMA Press, Inc./Alamy Stock Photo, **85** (c) Brian J. Skerry/National Geographic Creative, **87** (b) Fabrice Coffrini/Getty Images, **91** (c) Joel Sartore, National Geographic Photo Ark/National Geographic Creative, **92** (bl) Joel Sartore, National Geographic Photo Ark/National Geographic Creative, **92** (bc) Joel Sartore, National Geographic Photo Ark/National Geographic Creative, **92** (br) Joel Sartore/National Geographic Creative, **93** (c) Joel Sartore, National Geographic Photo Ark/National Geographic Creative, **95** (c) David Doubilet/National Geographic Creative, **96** (tl) © Mariana Fuentes, **96** (bc) Kent Kobersteen/National Geographic Creative, **97** (cr) David Doubilet/National Geographic Creative, **99** (t) Joel Sartore, National Geographic Photo Ark/National Geographic Creative, **100** (cr) Joel Sartore, National Geographic Photo Ark/National Geographic Creative, **102** (br) Ivy Close Images/Alamy Stock Photo, **103** (c) Joel Sartore, National Geographic Photo Ark/National Geographic Creative, **104** (t) Joel Sartore/National Geographic, **104** (bc) Joel Sartore, National Geographic Photo Ark/National Geographic Creative, **105** (t) Joel Sartore, National Geographic Photo Ark/National Geographic Creative, **105** (bc) Joel Sartore/National Geographic Creative, **107** (bc) Joel Sartore, National Geographic Photo Ark/National Geographic Creative, **109** (br) Joel Sartore, National Geographic Photo Ark/National Geographic Creative, **111** (c) 1001 Inventions Ltd, **112–113** (c) Robert Sisson/National Geographic, **113** (tr) Hulton Archive/Getty Images, **115** (t) 1001 Inventions Ltd, **116** (r) 1001 Inventions Ltd, **117** (b) Blaine Harrington III/Alamy Stock Photo, **118** (bc) 1001 Inventions Ltd, **119** (t) 1001 Inventions Ltd, **121** (cr) Michael Gottschalk/Getty Images, **122–123** (c) Peter Macdiarmid/Getty Images, **123** (tr) De Agostini Picture Library/Getty Images, **126** (br) Science & Society Picture Library/Getty Images, **129** (c) © Design Pics Inc./National Geographic Creative, **130–131** (c) NG MAPS/National Geographic, **131** (tr) NASA/CXC/MIT/F.K. Baganoff/National Geographic Stock, **131** (cr) © Babak Tafreshi/National Geographic Creative, **131** (br) © Michael Miller/Stocktrek Images/National Geographic Creative, **132** (b) oorka/Shutterstock, **133** (t) © NASA/JPL-Caltech, **134** (t) Martiniere Stephan/National Geographic Creative, **135** (c) © NASA/JPL-Caltech, **137** (t) © Wes Skiles/National Geographic Creative, **140** (tr) Getty Images/Getty Images, **140** (cr) © Paul Zahl/National Geographic Creative, **140** (br) © David Doubilet/National Geographic Creative, **140–141** (c) Brian J. Skerry/National Geographic Creative, **143** (b) NASA/Getty Images, **145** (bc) Babak Tafreshi/National Geographic Creative

Texts/Sources

2–3 Adapted from "Urban Explosion": NGM Nov 2002; 2016 data source: "The World's Cities in 2016": United Nations Data Booklet; **5–6** Adapted from "The Face of Seven Billion": http://ngm.nationalgeographic.com/2011/03/age-of-man/face-interactive; **8** Based on information from "World Population Prospects": Unit Nations 2015; **12–13** Based on information from "Global Web Index 2016" and "Nielsen Social Media Report 2016"; **20–21** Based on information from https://blog.linkedin.com/2012/11/15/dream_jobs; **24–25** Adapted from "Barrington Irving": http://www.nationalgeographic.com/explorers/bios/barrington-irving; **30–31** Adapted from "Emily Ainsworth": http://www.nationalgeographic.com/explorers/bios/emily-ainsworth; "Behind the Mexican Circus": http://voices.nationalgeographic.com/2012/05/23/behind-the-mexican-circus-with-young-explorer-emily-ainsworth; "Explorer of the Week": http://voices.nationalgeographic.com/2012/08/29/explorer-of-the-week-emily-ainsworth; **39** Based on information from "The No Regrets Travel List": https://www.contiki.com/ap/en/no-regrets-travel-list; **41** Adapted from "Adventurer Alastair Humphreys": http://www.nationalgeographic.com/adventure/features/adventurers-of-the-year/2012/alastair-humphreys; **56–57** Based on information from "Is Photography Dead?": https://digital-photography-school.com/history-photography; **59–60** Based on information from "So You Want to Be Successful on Instagram?": http://voices.nationalgeographic.com/2015/07/22/so-you-want-to-be-successful-on-instagram; **66–67** Based on information from "14 Not-Fake Shark Pictures From a Real Nat Geo Photographer": http://news.nationalgeographic.com/2016/12/shark-pictures-not-fake-brain-skerry/; **77–78** Based on information from "Teenage Brains": http://ngm.nationalgeographic.com/2011/10/teenage-brains/dobbs-text; "Are You a Risk Taker": http://ngm.nationalgeographic.com/2011/10/teenage-brains/risk-quiz; "Fear Factor: Success and Risk in Extreme Sports": http://news.nationalgeographic.com/news/2004/07/0709_040709_sciencerisk; **84–85** Adapted from "Brian Skerry": http://www.nationalgeographic.com/contributors/s/photographer-brian-skerry; "Could This 15-Year-Old Redefine Rock Climbing?": http://www.nationalgeographic.com/adventure/adventurers-of-the-year/2017/ashima-shiraishi-sport-climber-boulderer; "14 Year Old Achieves Hardest Boulder Climb Ever Done by a Woman": http://adventureblog.nationalgeographic.com/2016/03/22/14-year-old-ashima-shiraishi-climbs-hardest-boulder-problem-ever-done-by-a-woman; "Rock Climbing Prodigy Injured in Climbing Accident": http://www.nationalgeographic.com/adventure/activities/climbing/rock-climber-ashima-shiraishi-injured-in-fall; **95–95** Based on information from "Mariana Fuentes": http://www.nationalgeographic.com/explorers/bios/mariana-fuentes and additional information from "Protecting Sea Turtles From Climate Change Should Include Nesting Site Protection": http://www.redorbit.com/news/science/1112786409/sea-turtle-conservation-efforts-nesting-site-protection-021913; **101** Based on information from "Mass Extinctions": http://www.nationalgeographic.com/science/prehistoric-world/mass-extinction; **102–103** Based on information from http://www.joelsartore.com; **115–116** Based on information from: "1001 Inventions: The Enduring Legacy of Muslim Civilization," published by National Geographic Books, 2012; **122–123** Adapted from "Ada Lovelace Day Celebrates Women in Science": http://voices.nationalgeographic.com/2012/10/16/ada-lovelace-day; **133–134** Based on information from "Crazy Far": http://ngm.nationalgeographic.com/2013/01/125-space-exploration/folger-text and additional information from "NASA Telescope Reveals Largest Batch of Earth-Size, Habitable-Zone Planets Around Single Star": https://www.nasa.gov/press-release/nasa-telescope-reveals-largest-batch-of-earth-size-habitable-zone-planets-around; **140–141** Adapted from "Sea Mounts": http://ngm.nationalgeographic.com/2012/09/seamounts/stone-text

Maps and Infographics

2–3, **12–13**, **20–21**, **48–49**, **56–57** 5W Infographics; **48–49** Base map © maproom.net; **130–131** NG Maps/National Geographic

INDEX OF EXAM SKILLS AND TASKS

The activities in *Pathways Reading, Writing, and Critical Thinking* develop key reading skills needed for success on standardized exams such as TOEFL® and IELTS. In addition, many of the activities provide useful exam practice because they are similar to common question types in these tests.

Key Reading Skills	IELTS	TOEFL®	Page(s)
Recognizing vocabulary from context	✓	✓	7, 14, 26, 32, 42, 61, 80, 86, 106, 142
Recognizing main ideas	✓	✓	7, 14, 26, 32, 42, 44, 50, 61, 68, 79, 97, 106, 117, 124, 135
Scanning for details	✓	✓	7, 8, 32, 142
Making inferences	✓	✓	26
Recognizing pronoun references		✓	118

Common Question Types	IELTS	TOEFL®	Page(s)
Multiple choice	✓	✓	26, 42, 44, 46, 68, 79, 82, 86, 97, 100, 135, 138
Completion (notes, diagram, summary)	✓		7, 61, 86, 97, 117, 124, 135, 136, 138, 142
Short answer	✓		14, 28, 68, 98, 106
Matching tasks (headers, features, information)	✓		14, 50, 64, 79, 97, 106, 120, 135
True / False	✓		68
Prose summary		✓	61, 117, 124
Reference		✓	118
Rhetorical purpose		✓	50, 124, 138

Pathways Reading, Writing, and Critical Thinking also develops key writing skills needed for exam success. At *Foundations* level, the activities target sentence-level writing. As a result, they do not directly mirror writing tasks in TOEFL® or IELTS (which require students to write essays or other long pieces). However, the skills provide an important foundation for the longer writing tasks practiced in higher levels of the series.

Key Writing Skills	Page(s)
Writing effective sentences	15, 16, 17, 34, 53, 54, 69, 71, 88, 90, 110, 127, 128
Expressing and supporting opinions	51, 128, 143, 144, 146
Giving reasons and examples	72, 106, 107, 108, 110, 128, 138, 142, 146
Paraphrasing ideas and information	32, 68, 124, 142
Making comparisons	14, 32, 86, 100, 106, 120, 124, 138, 142

Pathways	CEFR	IELTS Band	TOEFL® Score
Level 4	C1	6.5–7.0	81–100
Level 3	B2	5.5–6.0	51–80
Level 2	B1–B2	4.5–5.0	31–50
Level 1	A2–B1	0–4.0	0–30
Foundations	**A1–A2**		